W9-CCT-841

HRMagazine™

GUIDE TO MANAGING PEOPLE

HRMagazine™

GUIDE TO MANAGING PEOPLE

Society for Human Resource Management
Alexandria, Virginia
USA

www.shrm.org

Edited by
Lauren Keller Johnson

This publication is designed to provide accurate and authoritative information regarding the subject matter covered. It is sold with the understanding that neither the publisher nor the authors nor the editor is engaged in rendering legal or other professional service. If legal advice or other expert assistance is required, the services of a competent, licensed professional should be sought. The federal and state laws discussed in this book are subject to frequent revision and interpretation by amendments or judicial revisions that may significantly affect employer or employee rights and obligations. Readers are encouraged to seek legal counsel regarding specific policies and practices in their organizations.

This book is published by the Society for Human Resource Management (SHRM©). The interpretations, conclusions and recommendations in this book are those of the authors and do not necessarily represent those of SHRM.

©2006 Society for Human Resource Management. All rights reserved.

This publication may not be reproduced, stored in a retrieval system, or transmitted in whole or in part, in any form or by any means, electronic, mechanical, photocopying, recording, or otherwise, without the prior written permission of the Society for Human Resource Management, 1800 Duke Street, Alexandria, VA 22314.

The Society for Human Resource Management (SHRM) is the world's largest association devoted to human resource management. Representing more than 210,000 individual members, the Society serves the needs of HR professionals by providing the most essential and comprehensive set of resources available. As an influential voice, SHRM is committed to advancing the human resource profession to ensure that HR is an essential and effective partner in developing and executing organizational strategy. Visit SHRM Online at www.shrm.org.

Library of Congress Cataloging-in-Publication Data

HR magazine guide to managing people / edited by Lauren Keller Johnson.

    p. cm.

Includes index.

ISBN-13: 978-1-58644-091-6

ISBN-10: 1-58644-091-8

1. Personnel management. 2. Personnel management--United States. I. Johnson, Lauren Keller. II. Society for Human Resource Management (U.S.) III. HRMagazine.

HF5549.H656 2007

658.3--dc22

2006032771

Edited by: Lauren Keller Johnson

Cover design by: Matt Hlubny

Printed by: United Book Press, Inc.

Index by: Lauren Keller Johnson

Interior design by: Matt Hlubny

Printed in the United States of America.

10 9 8 7 6 5 4 3 2 1

Contents

HRMagazine™

GUIDE TO MANAGING PEOPLE

Introduction

As business has grown more competitive than ever, managers in every function—including human resources—have come under increasing pressure to produce valuable results for their organizations quickly, reliably and cost-effectively.

In short, all of your company's managers are expected to "do more with less" by extracting maximum value from your teams. Managers are busier than before, and the challenges seem ever more daunting. Hiring the best talent, managing increased diversity in the workplace, motivating people to give their best on the job—these are just a few examples of the key responsibilities managers today are expected to fulfill with unprecedented skill.

We've compiled this anthology to help you not only tackle these and other challenges in your own human resources function—but also to aid you in training and educating other managers in your organization so they get the most from their teams.

This volume provides a wealth of practical guidelines for handling the toughest human resource issues. In addition to tactics for recruiting talented employees, leveraging employee diversity and motivating workers to excel, you'll find potent suggestions for honing employees' skills, assessing their performance and addressing problem behavior in teams. Additional sections cover strategies for managing contingent workers and for communicating effectively with employees.

The material in this book originally appeared as articles in the Society for Human Resource Management's (SHRM's) *HR Magazine*, the premier magazine focusing on the professional practice of human resources. These articles were edited for the Managing Smart feature on SHRM's web site (available to SHRM members online).

Now we're bringing you the best of these gems in one quick, easy volume. But we've done more than just organize the highest-quality articles into themed sections. We've also provided hands-on tools and information to help you apply the material in the articles. Here's a preview of the tools you'll find throughout the volume:

- **"QuickTips"** at the end of each section distill core lessons from each article in that section—providing a handy reference guide to the best practices offered by the article authors.

- **"Did You Know?"** boxes capture provocative facts and statistics offered in specific selections and relating to HR topics such as workforce demographics and employee attitudes.

- **Worksheets** enable you to document important information and action plans for addressing a crucial HR issue identified in an article. For example, one worksheet helps managers to record patterns of absenteeism that may indicate abuse of company policy and to lay out steps for dealing with the problem.

- **Self-assessments** help managers identify their strengths and areas for improvement. For instance, one self-assessment invites respondents to identify how well they motivate their employees—and to consider how they might strengthen weak areas. Another self-assessment gauges managers' effectiveness as listeners.

- **Checklists** help managers prepare to deal with a particular HR task outlined in an article. To illustrate, one checklist lays out required criteria for a memo reprimanding or terminating an employee. Another checklist enables managers to ensure that all the elements are in place for a job-sharing situation to succeed.

- **How-totables** provide specific techniques for dealing with unique HR challenges. For example, one table suggests management techniques to use with employees from diverse cultures. Another table offers ideas for choosing the right communication style at the right time (for instance, to create a stronger sense of camaraderie in a team).

We encourage you to use the tools in this book liberally. We hope you'll give the book to your managers so that they can use the articles, "Quick Tips," "Did You Know?" boxes and how-to tables. And we hope that you keep the book handy at your desks and take pen or pencil in hand to fill out the worksheets, checklists and self-assessments. The more the tools are used, the more valuable they become.

SHRM members can access all of these Managing Smart articles in chronological order in Word format free of charge. To see the Managing Smart feature on SHRM's web site, go to www.shrm.org/managingsmart. To see articles from *HR Magazine* go to www.shrm.org/hrmagazine.

SECTION ONE: RECRUITING TALENTED EMPLOYEES

Your organization can't fulfill its mission and leave rivals scrambling unless it attracts top talent. Yet recruiting skilled, dedicated employees will grow tougher than ever—thanks to demographic changes such as mass retirement of baby boomers. And finding the right talent to match your organization is more difficult than ever.

How to prevail in the war for talent? The articles in this section offer potent strategies—everything from asking employees to interview promising candidates who would be their peers to interviewing technical candidates and getting the most from reference checks.

Try "Peer Interviewing" to Find the Perfect Candidate for Your Team
By Martha Frase-Blunt

Imagine being able to handpick your co-workers. The result might be a stronger, more cohesive team that shares the company's culture. That's just one of the many benefits of peer interviewing—a selection process that allows members of the work group to help evaluate job candidates.

Peer interviewing provides companies with a lot of payback, including a higher degree of acceptance for a candidate, a higher degree of retention and a better brand recognition about your process, says Jeremy Eskenazi, who's been helping companies implement this technique for more than 15 years. Now the managing principal of Riviera Advisors, a Long Beach, Calif., HR consulting firm, he believes that peer interviewing is a critical element of building a cohesive company culture.

Eskenazi endorses a 360-degree process in which peers, supervisors and subordinates interview candidates either through a series of one-on-one interviews or as a panel. Eskenazi recommends no more than four interviewers and that each be assigned one dimension on which to concentrate. For example, one person might be responsible for a skills assessment, another would interview for culture fit, and so on. Other dimensions might include programming and logic skills (for technical positions), background and past experiences, the candidate's interest in the company and leadership skills (for management candidates).

Some of these dimensions can be combined into a single interview to reduce the number of meetings, says Eskenazi. And by having each interviewer focus on something different, you reduce the chance that the candidate will be asked the same questions again and again and feel compelled to give similar responses each time.

To select an interviewing team, look for a cross section of employees who reflect diversity, age, race, etc., as well as differences in thought and maturity. "Blend newcomers with old-timers," says Eskenazi. "For large companies, it makes sense to include peers from the same team or work group of the position being filled. Smaller companies are free to mix it up across divisions." He also believes it's essential to designate a coordinating "point person" to oversee the process.

"This individual should be one who does not 'own' the position," says Eskenazi, but rather one who can oversee the process in an unbiased way. "When an interviewer needs to pass information or questions up the line to the next interviewer, for example, this communication can be handled by the coordinator." He also advises not having interviewers speak directly to each other during the process; those who haven't met the candidate need to remain open-minded. Suggested questions or information for other interviewers should be directed to the point person.

Cary Smith, senior recruiter at textbook publishers Holt, Rinehart and Winston in Austin, Texas, conducts team interviews for virtually every position in his company. He believes it's helped the company reduce its attrition rate by 70 percent. "We better understand who would fit into our culture, what they bring to the table and how we can attract them to the company," says Smith. "A traditional behavioral interview only predicts success half the time. But a team can create a more cohesive opinion together, working through the issues instead of having one individual form a singular opinion to project on the candidate."

Holt, Rinehart and Winston uses the panel interview approach. After the hiring manager conducts initial phone screens, promising candidates are scheduled for a one-and-a-half to two-hour interview. The panel is made up of three to four team members selected because of their job knowledge, but they also tend to be people with the longest tenure who are, in a sense, the keepers of the culture. Smith also likes to include a senior executive when higher-level candidates are questioned.

Before the meeting, panel interviewers have individually selected specific questions from a 65-point questionnaire Smith developed. "Each team member sorts through this large list of attitudes or behaviors, picking the top 10 he or she feels are most important to be successful in this particular position. We try to make it very simple for the interviewers," adds Smith. "They have plenty of work of their own to do, so we try to streamline the process for them."

Smith also schedules the interviews for one day and expects the team to make an immediate decision. "We find it's important for the group to gather right after the panel when thoughts are fresh," says Smith. "We capture the feedback right away, giving the team an hour and a half to make a decision."

Riviera Advisors recommends giving interviewers just four choices: strongly recommend, recommend, don't recommend and strongly don't recommend. They also should expect to explain their reasoning to the group. "We've found that people change their minds if given too much time to decide; they are influenced by others' assessments," says Eskenazi.

But this isn't a democracy, Eskenazi adds. "The hiring manager has to have the final say, backed up by HR. Otherwise the process bogs down." This lack of democracy can be a difficult sell to the interviewing team if not handled correctly, he warns. "You want to engage the team and [to] give them ownership of the process, but you have to communicate very clearly why the final decision is being made. And you have to be prepared for backlash if this isn't done effectively."

Many companies also provide interview training to every employee who might be involved in peer interviewing, such as learning how to develop an effective position profile, what constitutes illegal questions and how to avoid revealing proprietary information about the company. Both Eskenazi's and Smith's training programs feature mock interviews. "This helps the team understand each other's style and identifies questions that go down the rabbit hole or that reveal personal agendas," says Smith.

One caveat: Peer interviewing is not suitable in every situation. "It's not ideal for a replacement search for someone who was asked to leave," says Eskenazi. "There's too much emotion involved." And while he doesn't necessarily endorse excluding executive candidates, he believes they may feel less comfortable jumping through so many hoops.

Put Substance before Style during Hiring Interviews
By Laura Gassner Otting

Are you letting your first impressions get the best of you when you're interviewing job applicants? Most likely. As many as four out of five hiring decisions are made within the first 10 minutes of an interview, according to some studies. Those decisions are based on little more than the applicant's clothing or hairstyle, a subconscious stereotype or a preconceived notion about a particular candidate or type of candidate.

Indeed, the first impressions of hiring managers in initial interviews may drive the entire hiring process because managers expect—and perceive—better answers from candidates who make a favorable first impression. Similarly, responses from candidates whose first impressions are disappointing can be received much less favorably if they were expected to have made a better impression.

"Once an impression is formed and the potential candidate has been accepted or rejected, additional information that goes against the impression carries less weight in evaluating a candidate's ability to do the job," says Lois Lindauer, president of Lois L. Lindauer Searches in Boston. That leads managers to make hiring decisions based on style over substance—and pass over highly qualified candidates.

Managers particularly need to be aware of how body language, posture, facial expressions and eye contact drive more than half of first impressions, according to psychological studies. Such cues send us signals about a candidate's preparation, confidence and even grooming habits. Moreover, studies show that attractive people are implicitly seen by interviewers as having better personalities, higher intelligence, more poise and greater honesty, just as neat people are presumed to be efficient, punctual and detail-oriented.

That's why it is so important for hiring-managers to avoid presumptions. For example, the presumption that a candidate who arrives late has a tardiness problem is fundamentally flawed. Forming negative impressions about candidates who may have been caught in situations out of their control—or positive impressions about candidates because they're attractive—can be self-serving.

Although it's important to note personal traits—such as honesty, integrity, determination and humor—to determine whether a candidate would succeed at the job in question, an interview should focus on the candidate's professional experience—his or her track record of on-the-job performance.

One way to do that? Suspend judgments, says Gale Batchelder, vice president of the Boston-based executive search firm Auerbach Associates. "Sometimes something about a person really turns me off—their looks, their clothes, whatever," she says. "Or I feel really attracted to someone's intellect or humor or looks and then view them favorably right away. I have to remind myself constantly to suspend immediate judgments until I learn more."

Another idea is to put first impressions in their place—one piece of the puzzle, says Susan Egmont, founder of Egmont Associates, an executive search firm in Boston. "It's perfectly legitimate to see what first impression is presented, and to eliminate or select candidates because generally they show you the best foot they have to put forward," she says. "However, the first impression just can't be the only criteria. If a person is late or doesn't present well but has potential, then obviously a second interview is in order, or at least a conversation about what you suspect didn't come out sufficiently can be a good test. Then good reference checking can bear out or deny the candidate's own assertions."

Another factor to consider is your own decision-making style. Do you react instinctively, or do you take time to deliberate? The odds are that your interviewing style mirrors your decision-making style. "One way to guard against this is to be aware of it," says Batchelder. By developing an awareness of what kind of people you are drawn to, and why, you can evaluate whether that has worked for you in the past, she explains. Ask yourself:

- What were my first impressions of other people I hired?

- When did that work for me and when did it lead me astray?

"In many instances, our intuitions are right, and we should heed them," says Batchelder. "But we all have blind spots that cause us to react negatively or positively that then lead us to certain expectations."

By understanding one's own behavior and the demands of the open job, a hiring manager can interview more objectively, says Lindauer. "Taking an immediate liking to a person should trigger tougher questions by you. Conversely, you should work harder to engage more with those who don't initially impress you." An interviewer who has a negative impression of a candidate often does the opposite, spending most of the interview disengaged or tearing the candidate apart through overly tough questions or a combative attitude. To keep the interview fair, remember that it takes at least 10 minutes for a candidate to get past his or her own nervousness and for the hiring manager or interviewing committee to establish a flow of conversation. Suspending judgment at least until a rapport is established is the most effective way to begin to see candidates for what they truly bring to the table.

Past performance is the most important indicator of a candidate's possible success in his or her next position, so questions based on past performance are often the best way to determine suitability for a position. Good interview questions start with a good job description, one that outlines what the successful candidate is expected to accomplish on the job. Using the job description, you should create a list of question areas based not on the candidate's résumé but on the qualifications and track record a candidate must bring to the job to succeed in the position.

Although candidates differ from one another in experience and personality, the job description does not change. Questions may be tailored slightly to accommodate individual candidates and their experience, but it's important to have a predetermined list of topics to ensure that candidates are being evaluated against the same benchmarks.

David Haley, of the Boston-based search firm Isaacson, Miller, advises hiring managers and search committees to think of themselves as juries. First, they should take all of the evidence into consideration before reaching a verdict, and, second, they need to act as if the applicant is a good candidate until he or she proves otherwise. "Never fall in love with a candidate," cautions Haley. "It's OK to have strong feelings about a candidate; most hiring managers do. It is not OK to allow these feelings to get in the way of the decision-making process until they are weighed against all of the evidence." The evidence, Haley explains, should include formal and informal opinions and many reference checks.

Second opinions help, too. Egmont says, "Having a hiring committee rather than a single person can guard against one person's energy level flagging if the first impression isn't strong for them. If the whole committee isn't interested after the first impression, follow the wisdom of the group and make the interview respectful but shorter than planned."

Finally, know your own biases, and commit to work actively to change or challenge them. Some tools can be helpful. For example, conducting interviews by telephone can minimize the effect of first impressions, allowing the interviewer to be influenced more by substance than by style. Like references, checklists and committee interviews, telephone interviews help an interviewer to avoid jumping to an immediate conclusion about a candidate's value and force that interviewer to hear more about what a candidate has to say than how he or she might say it.

Use the following tips to help you avoid being unduly influenced by distracting and potentially incorrect first impressions and learn more about the candidate's track record:

- Examine your decision-making style. Do you react instinctively, or do you ponder before making up your mind? Are you diplomatic or adversarial in your approach? Where has your style served you or failed you in the past?

- Let your fingers do the walking. Screen all candidates with a telephone interview before setting up an in-person interview. Delay the effects of any visual first impressions by ascertaining vital information in a less loaded environment.

- Listen to others first. Take time to do one or two preliminary reference checks before meeting a candidate. Push yourself to see the candidate through the eyes of his or her references, of the person's next manager and your own.

- Treat everyone equally. Go into the interview with a list of questions or topics based on the performance indicators in the job description. You may depart from the list as a candidate's skills or experience demand, but ask the same qualifications-centered questions of all candidates.

- Create a warm-up period. Put everyone at ease by chatting casually at the start of the interview, offering a beverage and allowing the candidate to, say, remove a suit jacket if he or she wishes.

- Remember that past is prologue. Ask the candidate for stories about successes or failures specifically relevant to the goals set forth in the job in question. Avoid questions that start with "What would you do if ... ."

- Test your fallibility. Throw some hardball questions at likeable candidates and softer ones at the candidates you don't like. Remember that their interview performance may be based on what they perceive you doing.

- Set up a self-check. Note the halfway point of your scheduled time; re-evaluate your impressions.

- Get a second opinion. Interview as a committee to reduce personal dynamics, or bring in potential supervisors or staff members to balance your personal biases.

- Listen more than you talk. The candidate should do more talking than you do.

Did You Know?

- Four out of five hiring decisions are made within the first 10 minutes of an interview.

- Body language, posture, facial expressions and eye contact drive more than half of first impressions.

- It takes at least 10 minutes for a job candidate to get past his or her own nervousness, and for the hiring manager or interviewing committee to establish a flow of conversation.

- Past performance is the most important indicator of a candidate's possible success in his or her next position.

Focus on Career Progression to Find Win-Win Hires
By Paul Falcone

Getting to really know job candidates gets trickier and trickier these days, thanks to job-finding guides and online career strategy resources that encourage applicants to tailor their résumés and responses to each employer. Similarly, employers have their own arsenal of interview questioning books and HR courses that help them try to gain the upper hand. In essence, the interviewing game is stepped up on both sides—but it's not clear that anyone benefits. Maybe it's time to simplify interviewing on both sides so that the interview itself becomes an exercise of value rather than a game of wits, strategies and defenses. By turning your current interviewing style—as sophisticated as it may be—into a more open and honest dialogue, you can focus as much on the candidate's needs as on the needs of your company. Key to this strategy is to discover the links in a candidate's career progression.

The reasons for leaving past positions provide an understanding of the candidate's values, motivations and career goals. Each reason for leaving a prior company should be fulfilled by the next company on the individual's résumé. That's how people build careers and justify the chain of jobs they've held: They look for greater responsibilities, title changes, new technical skills, lateral experience and, sometimes, simply more money. Candidates who successfully articulate how these various factors have led to this point in their careers add a contextual and historical framework to what you see on their résumé.

What's critical now is the individual's current reason for leaving his or her present job. Can that reason be fulfilled by your company? Does your opportunity fill a short-term need and also make sense for the individual over the long haul? If not, the candidate may be pursuing a strategy of "change for change's sake," which will typically lead to premature turnover. To gain a better understanding of a candidate's motivation, ask, "What's your primary reason for leaving your current company, and how would joining us fill that need?" Likewise, you could ask, "What would joining our firm do for you in terms of adding new skills and building your résumé?" As an alternative, try this: "If you were to accept this position with us today, how would you explain that to a prospective employer five years from now? How would this job provide a link in your future career progression?"

In the same way, be sure to challenge the two most overused excuses for leaving a former position. "No room for growth" may be a legitimate reason for leaving the candidate's current company, but qualify the real meaning behind that superficial response by asking, "What does growth mean to you? Is it a vertical climb up the corporate ladder, a lateral move that broadens your overall skills, or is money more of a motivator for you at this point? And it's OK to be very straightforward in your response; there's no right or wrong answer here."

Similarly, being laid off may be a legitimate reason for leaving a past position as well, but be sure to qualify the layoff. Too many people out there are "individually laid off," which may mean that the company chose to eliminate the position rather than proceed down the path of progressive discipline due to poor performance. You can qualify the layoff by asking questions such as, "How many people were laid off at the same time as you? How many waves of layoffs did you survive before you, yourself, were cut? Did they ever back-fill your position after you left?"

Challenging the layoff response also may provide interesting insights into the individual. For example, if she was individually laid off on more than one occasion and you can't get any references from prior employers, it may be a sign that she has ongoing performance problems. On the other hand, if she was asked to "turn off the lights" as the last person standing at the time of the company's liquidation, it could tell you a lot about her trustworthiness and loyalty.

When it comes to employed candidates who may be considering a lateral move into your company, be sure to ask, "What would have to change at your current company for you to consider staying?" As a rule, people join companies and leave managers, meaning the initial appeal to join a firm is derived from an individual's perception of a company—its brand-name reputation, culture and the like. On the other hand, the difference between an active job seeker and a passive job seeker may be one bad day in the office. The mental break that triggers a job search typically comes from frustrations with a manager's leadership style or from lack of promotional opportunities. To get beyond those frustrations, follow up with this question: "What would be your next move in career progression if you stayed put?"

To get behind the candidate's criteria for selecting a company, ask him to detail three or four criteria he is using to select his next job or company. People are typically interested in changing jobs for one of three reasons: the company they seek to join in terms of its image and reputation; the position they're applying for in terms of its uniqueness, variety and interest level; and the people they'd work with as far as the camaraderie, teamwork and open communication. After that opening question, ask "What are the top five companies that you would pursue right now if you could?" Similarly, say, "Tell me the titles of the positions you would plan on pursuing in these companies." Also, you might ask, "Are there any other pending offers on the table or late-stage interviewing discussions that are in play?" Most candidates will be a little thrown off by your self-assessment questions because they may have never had to articulate these details to a prospective employer on an interview, but it will open the door to the bonding relationship you're seeking to develop.

Discovering the Thinking Behind a Candidate's Career Choices

If the candidate ...	Ask...
Is currently employed	• "What's your primary reason for wanting to leave your current company? And how would joining us fill that need?"
Cites "no room for growth" as reason for job-hunting	• "What does growth mean to you? Is it a vertical climb up the corporate ladder? A lateral move that broadens your skills? An increase in compensation?"
Is considering a lateral move into your company	• "What would have to change at your current company for you to consider staying?" • "What would be your next move in career progression if you stayed with your current company?"
Is interviewing with multiple potential employers	• "What three or four criteria are you using to select your next job?" • "What are the top five companies you would pursue right now if you could? Tell me the titles of the positions you would pursue in these companies." • "Are there any other pending offers on the table or late-stage interviewing discussions in play?"

Be Honest When Selling Potential Hires on Your Business
By Carolyn Brandon

Are you putting your company's real face forward when recruiting potential employees? The image an employer projects for potential hires, also known as its recruitment brand, should, above all, be honest. Painting an unrealistic picture of your company or misrepresenting what employees should expect from your organization can be a huge mistake.

Job interviews can be like first dates where both parties put on an extra layer of sheen, embellishing their love of a certain sport or of foreign-language films. A few months later, after the honeymoon is over, one admits to hating football and the other fesses up to preferring action flicks. Soon, the relationship ends and everyone feels like time has been wasted. Similarly, when employers and potential candidates aren't honest with each other, bad decisions result.

So, how do you create an honest, successful recruitment brand for your company? Start with an accurate assessment and highlight your strengths, says Elizabeth Amorose, project director at the Carbone Smolan Agency (CSA), a New York-based marketing firm that specializes in recruitment strategies. Amorose encourages clients to develop a list of the top five to 10 messages they feel candidates must know. These should include any special advantages employees might gain by working for your organization, such as opportunities for advancement, the chance to help in an important cause, the opportunity to develop highly prized skills, the respect of working for an industry leader or the ability to reap generous benefits and perks.

Also, focus on what separates you from the competition. For example, Amorose recently worked on a recruitment campaign for the New York law firm Cadwalader, Wickersham and Taft. The firm contracted with CSA because executives did not believe its recruitment materials were effectively portraying the law firm's image, says Claudia Freeman, CSA's director of marketing and communications. Some new hires agreed, saying they could not attain the work/life balance portrayed in Cadwalader's recruitment materials. Instead, they were greeted with the same long hours and strict deadlines that are common to the legal profession. But what really sets Cadwalader apart from other law firms is that it offers client contact early in attorneys' tenure, which can help attorneys reach the next level in their careers, says Freeman. In a campaign called "The Real Deal," Amorose highlighted this advantage to Cadwalader's recruits, while being honest about the firm's expectations regarding the number of work hours per week.

When you interview job candidates, begin by giving a realistic job preview, recommends Maureen Henson, SPHR, director of recruitment and employment strategies for the Henry Ford Health System in Gross Isle, Mich. That involves thinking about organizational culture, or "the way we do things around here." Consider how decisions are made, how much authority employees have and how people are held accountable within the organization. It's also wise to show simple, real-life examples of the culture by letting the candidate meet peers and co-workers on all levels. Management candidates should meet with direct reports and peers, as well as upper management.

"Even if an employee involved in the selection process has a less-than-positive attitude or you fear they may say something unfavorable, this should not always deter you from involving them," says Henson. She also believes that current employees are best able to predict whether the candidate is a good fit for the environment because they are the ones living and working there day to day.

Experts agree that being comfortable in a culture is ultimately an individual decision. But being open with applicants can help them make informed decisions about whether to accept a position and where they feel they fit in.

How to Interview a Technical Candidate—When You're Not a Techie
By Paul Falcone

Even self-confident managers find it daunting to interview technical candidates. It's easy to feel vulnerable when you're responsible for interviewing, recommending or hiring technicians with expertise beyond your scope. Still, you'll probably have to do it—and make hire/no hire recommendations or decisions at some time in your career. Here's how:

Start by stating your knowledge limitations up front and asking candidates to evaluate themselves according to their own criteria. This spares you the embarrassment of pretending that you understand the technical nature of their job and should provide you with enough information to make an evaluative recommendation based on a candidate's self-analysis of his qualifications, potential of career progression and history of achievements and shortcomings.

Let's assume you're hiring a lab technician who is responsible for gene sequencing, an important role on your team. Here's how you might start the interview: "Laura, as a business manager in this unit, I focus more of my time on the behind-the-scenes administration of the lab. I've got my degree in microbiology, but I'm not as familiar with gene-sequencing techniques. I'd prefer if you answer my questions in layman's terms and teach me what you're doing by explaining it as if I've never had a day of biochemistry in my life. Would that be all right with you?"

Then, ask the candidate to evaluate herself according to her own criteria. You might begin with her current role: "Let's look first at gene sequencing, an important part of the position you're applying for in our lab. Tell me about the gene sequencing you're doing at your current organization. What exactly do you do now?"

You'll also want to be sure to ask candidates to talk about the challenges ahead in transitioning from their current companies to your organization based on differences in product lines, computer systems, research methodologies and the like. You might follow up your initial query with a question like this: "Your current lab focuses on the human genome project; our lab, as you know, does cancer genetics. What do you think you'd be doing differently from a gene-sequencing standpoint in our lab as opposed to what you do now in your current lab?"

Then, let the candidate help you assess her technical skills. Ask, "On a scale of 1 to 5, how do you rank yourself from a technical standpoint? In other words, if a '1' means you aren't very technically advanced in your field, and a '5' means you truly are 'leading edge' technically, how would you rank yourself?" Most candidates will rank themselves as a 3 or a 4, depending on their experience and level of comfort with the position for which they're interviewing. Few will rank themselves a 5 for fear of being perceived as cocky or arrogant. Once they rank themselves as a 3 or a 4, ask, "Why would you rank yourself that way?"

Finally, ask the logical follow-up query: "What would you add to your background to make you a 5?" At that point, you'll have enough information to measure the gap between the ideal credentials and this candidate's background. Still, to help you focus further on the issue of "technical match," ask another follow-up question: "Where would we need to give you the most support, direction and structure in your initial employment period to make sure that you excelled in this position from a technical point of view? What else should I know relative to how you see your qualifications for this position from a technical standpoint?"

Armed with this information, you should be able to confidently assess the candidate versus the position to either make the hiring decision or write a recommendation to a hiring manager/Ph.D. biochemist. Remember, supervisors aren't always expected to have the same level of technical competence as the people they hire—especially when you are talking about arcane fields of study. By focusing your interview on career progression potential and achievement profiles, you set the stage for counteroffer possibilities, reference checking and salary negotiations. Be sure, however, to be able to touch on the technical aspects of the interview enough to discuss your concerns or recommendations, ask relevant questions and come to an informed hiring decision.

It Takes More Than a Reference Check to Weed out Liars
By Pamela Babcock

If you're back in the hiring mode, beware: A substantial number of job candidates fudge the truth on résumés and job applications. ADP Screening and Selection Services, a unit of the Roseland, N.J.-based ADP payroll and benefits managing company, says of the 2.6 million background checks it performed in 2001, 44 percent of applicants lied about their work histories, 41 percent lied about their education and 23 percent falsified credentials or licenses.

Whether it's competition for jobs, continuing problems with corporate ethics or some other reason, it appears more people are lying about their qualifications—and that spells trouble for managers who screen job candidates inadequately. "One bad hire can just wreck an organization and create a legal and financial nightmare for a company," says Lester S. Rosen, an attorney and president of Employment Screening Resources in Novato, Calif. At a minimum, hiring a liar can burden you with the extra costs of recruiting, hiring and training that employee's replacement.

So, how do you maximize your chances of weeding out applicants who lie? First, be aware that you're unlikely to detect lies through body language. Fidgeting, stuttering or avoiding eye contact could simply be symptoms of nervousness about the interview rather than indicators of intent to deceive.

"Most people cannot tell from demeanor whether someone is lying or telling the truth—but most people think they can," says Paul Ekman, author of 13 books, including *Telling Lies* (W.W. Norton, 2001).

Over the years, Ekman has tested about 6,000 people—among them college students, police officers, judges, lawyers, psychiatrists and agents of the FBI, the CIA and the Drug Enforcement Administration—to determine if they can tell if someone is lying. He has found, he says, that "95 percent of them are close to chance—they'd do just as well flipping a coin."

Ekman's advice to managers: "Be cautious about your own judgments based on demeanor, and be cautious about people who claim that there are signs of lying that they can teach you quickly in this situation. The most important thing to know is you'd better not trust your intuition, because it's probably wrong."

Visual clues aside, if you suspect an applicant is lying, you can take further steps. First, compare what the person says with the information on résumés and applications. By asking pointed questions, you can make it harder for an applicant to construct a series of lies, says Phillip Maltin, an attorney specializing in employment and business litigation with K&R Law Group in Los Angeles.

"If you suspect someone is lying, never attack the big lie, but ask questions about the facts that surround it, focusing on details," Maltin says. Listen closely. If an applicant says "I supervised a staff of 100," or "I'm a turnaround artist who takes businesses from financial instability to financial success," ask for further details. Here are some other tips:

- Ask a candidate to describe a work experience as it relates to a specific job skill you are trying to evaluate.

- Take extensive notes, and follow up on inconsistencies or contradictions. Probe for details.

- Tell the candidate you'll need to verify the information, and ask for contact names.

Kevin Wilson, an HR consultant with PeopleResources.Net, a recruiting firm in Boston, says behavioral and situational interviewing may be useful if you suspect exaggeration. "I might say, 'Tell me the story of your last PowerPoint presentation and how you got through the steps and how you did it,'" Wilson says. "Obviously, if they've done one, it's pretty easy for them to tell you how they did it, and you can make a judgment whether it's valid." Or if an applicant claims to have supervised employees, use situational interviewing by asking, "How would you handle an irate employee?"

Background and reference checks are other common procedures that can unveil lies, but it's important to go beyond the obvious. An applicant's claim to possess a degree from a particular university can be checked easily with a phone call to the school, of course, but checking employment references can be more difficult because most companies refuse to provide anything but the basics. That's why managers need to pursue other avenues, such as calling peers, former employers, former supervisors who are no longer with the company, advises Mary Cheddie, SPHR, vice president of human resources for the Orvis Co., a Manchester, Vt., mail order sporting goods firm. "I also listen a lot to the unspoken words. Like if I ask, 'Would you rehire this employee?' and the person says, 'Ahh, umm.'"

One of the most effective ways to avoid hiring a liar or to preserve the right to fire one is to use a standard application, experts say. An application can state that supplying false information is grounds for not being hired or for dismissal. Also, the information given—or the information gaps—on applications can suggest productive lines of questioning in interviews or can provide reasons to drop the applicant right away. Warning signs include neglecting to sign the application, which could shield the candidate from being accused of falsification or not consenting to background screening, says Rosen. Other signals include not answering questions in the criminal record section, failing to explain periods of unemployment or reasons for leaving previous jobs and not providing enough information for reference checks.

Also, it's crucial to know the person's previous addresses because if you need to do a criminal record search on an applicant, you will have to do it at the courthouses serving the areas where the applicant has lived. There is no official national criminal database available to most private employers, leaving courthouse searches as your primary option. There are more than 10,000 courthouses across the country, and information on previous addresses can help you search effectively.

If an applicant appears to be lying, can managers simply drop the candidate and move on? A hiring decision based solely on a subjective impression that the person has lied—with no objective grounds or reasons offered to the applicant—may be hard for an employer to defend in a discriminatory hiring suit, Rosen says. "Without any third-party verification" that the person was lying, he says, "it can be a tough legal position." But Cheddie, at Orvis, says that as long as businesses abide by nondiscrimination laws, they have the right to choose the best-qualified applicants. "The company is the one who holds the cards," she says. "It's our decision if we believe somebody's lying."

Quick Tips for Recruiting Talented Employees

- Want to build stronger, cohesive teams? Ask several of your employees to evaluate job candidates for new positions in your department or team—looking particularly at skills, culture fit and interest in the company. One organization that uses "peer interviewing" reduced its attrition rate by 70 percent!

- Do you tend to allow first impressions of a job candidate to drive the entire hiring process? Avoid this all-too-common pitfall by suspending judgments about a candidate based on initial perceptions of characteristics such as his or her punctuality, posture, likability and attractiveness.

- How do you ensure that a job candidate's goals and needs align with your company's objectives? Use disciplined questions—such as "What's your primary reason for leaving your current company, and how would joining us fill that need?"—to uncover the reasoning behind previous job changes.

- Want to create an honest—and successful—"recruitment brand" for your company? Resist any urge to embellish the advantages of working for your organization to win a talented job candidate. For example, don't soft-pedal the long work hours people put in. Instead, articulate the special advantages employees might gain by working for the company, for instance, advancement opportunities, the chance to help in an important cause or the opportunity to develop highly prized skills.

- Planning to interview a technical candidate—and you're not a "techie" yourself? State your knowledge limitations up front and ask the candidate to rate his or her technical competency according to the person's own criteria. Invite the candidate to explain his or her thinking behind the ratings, and ask how your company could best enable the person to excel in the open position from a technical point of view.

- Want to weed out job applicants who are lying about their qualifications? Ask pointed questions about a claim that you think may be untrue or exaggerated. For example, "You said you're competent with PowerPoint. Tell me about your last PowerPoint presentation—how you got through the steps and did the work."

SECTION TWO:
MANAGING DIVERSITY

Few managers disagree that a diverse workforce gives an organization crucial competitive advantages—such as more creative ideas for solving problems and serving new and existing markets. Yet when people from different cultural backgrounds come together in the workplace, misunderstanding and outright conflict can crop up.

How to manage differences so you maximize the value promised by diversity? This section offers helpful advice—including understanding the unique characteristics of numerous cultures and knowing how to interact with diverse employees in ways that are compatible with their cultural background.

Savvy Managers Tune in to Cultural Differences
By Lee Gardenswartz and Anita Rowe

In today's diverse workplaces, employees bring a wide range of cultural backgrounds that influence how close they stand to others, how loud they speak, how they deal with conflict—even how they participate in meetings. It's not surprising, then, that these culturally varying backgrounds can lead to misinterpretations of behavior, as well as conflict.

Consider the norm of hierarchy and status. As managers, we want everyone to feel valued and to participate in solving problems and making decisions. But being honest and offering ideas may be difficult for an employee who has been taught deference to age, gender or title because he doesn't want to be seen in the position of challenging the authority of an elder or boss.

Along with the norm of hierarchy and status, other important cultural norms that influence behavior are:

- Group versus individual orientation.

- Time consciousness.

- Communication.

- Conflict resolution.

For example, time-conscious managers may mistakenly view people whose cultures take a more relaxed view toward deadlines as being less committed to team goals, as well as less dependable, accountable and reliable. Or, consider the employee who nods "yes" but doesn't mean it. This individual may be simply operating according to his norm of communication in which one never says "no" to a boss.

At the same time, managers who are direct communicators expect a "tell-it-like-it-is" response from their subordinates. But when these employees are indirect communicators, they expect managers to read the contextual clues to understand their responses. In these cases, managers may need to hone their skills to pick up on nonverbal cues that may indicate when nodding and affirmative response are polite, face-saving gestures, not indications of agreement or understanding.

As you can see, it's important for managers to recognize the role that culture plays in interactions and to try to identify the critical elements of the cultures involved. Once you identify your preferences and expectations, you then can focus on the norms and preferences of your employees. Noting the cultural and preferential differences will help you avoid interpreting the behavior of your employees through the prism of your own cultural background.

Once you've identified the differences, you can search for alternate approaches that are more compatible with an employee's cultural background to get the information and effective communication you need. Here are some suggestions:

- Avoid yes/no questions, such as, "Is that clear?" or "Do you understand?" Instead, give the employee options from which to choose. Ask for specific information, such as, "Which step will you do first with this new procedure?"

- If time allows, perform the task along with the employee or watch to see how well he understands your directions.

- Try using passive language that focuses on the situation or behavior, rather than the individual. For example, instead of saying, "You must answer calls by the third ring," say, "Calls must be answered by the third ring."

- Give employees enough time to collect their thoughts before a meeting so they can feel prepared to bring input.

- Have employees work in small groups, generating ideas through discussion and presenting input as a group.

One of the most important functions of a manager is developing and grooming employees for promotion. Cross-cultural norms have a huge impact on this task because of the underlying assumptions a manager might make about an employee's potential. To determine promotion potential, managers consider questions such as:

- How is initiative demonstrated?

- What behaviors show commitment?

- How much is high potential determined by accomplishing the task and how much is determined by good interpersonal skills?

- How do employees use and showcase their unique talents?

In answering these questions, managers who are aware of cultural differences will make fewer assumptions about the motivations and drive of certain employees. For example, "initiative" won't necessarily be defined as acting without waiting for directions but will be defined as the ability to keep the group moving, to make some contribution and to help preserve harmony in the face of expected differences. "Commitment" may not be defined strictly in terms of meeting deadlines but also as encouraging further exploration of an issue or being more creative or flexible in striving to get the best outcome.

Managers who are aware of different cultural norms also are less likely to incorrectly interpret behaviors and prescribe ineffective courses of action when developing people. Toward this end, here are some suggestions for managers to consider:

- Teach employees to interpret the culture of the organization by pointing out factors such as how people dress, recreational patterns and the formality or informality of communication. Employees can make effective choices when they clearly understand the informal rules of the organizational culture.

- Help employees understand the difference between deadlines that are nonnegotiable and those that are more elastic.

- Get an accurate sense of the person's planning and organizational skills. Then, set clear expectations that help the employee perform better and build in follow-up sessions.

- Coach employees who are uncomfortable acknowledging their own individual work to talk about accomplishments through work group performance. As employees try to move up, the need to sell oneself in an unassuming way as part of a work group is a comfortable way to show one's part in a group's accomplishment.

- Focus on relationship building. An employee can learn that giving a manager feedback is an act of loyalty and help. But this is a paradigm shift that requires rapport, safety and trust.

Conflict is difficult to manage for most of us, and it becomes more so when employees and managers have different rules about how to handle it. Some employees will prefer direct discussion of differences. Others will find this approach upsetting and disruptive. In addition, differences in attitudes toward status may influence how people deal with conflict.

Managers need to help employees recognize these differences and encourage them to share their preferences with each other. This proactive approach helps build a common base of understanding about the best ways to deal with each other. Here are some specific steps to resolve conflict in culturally appropriate ways:

- Hold team development sessions where employees can learn more about their own and each other's styles and preferences in terms of conflicts.

- In one-on-one sessions, help employees understand cultural differences that may underlie the conflicts they are experiencing.

- Consider using a third-party intermediary to help resolve conflict in a face-saving manner.

- Create a norm that says conflict is a normal part of any workplace and that resolving it requires give and take on all sides.

- Work to create solution strategies that meet both your objectives and those of your employees.

Culture Differences Influence Expectations of Managers
By Dianne Nilsen, Brenda Kowske and Kshanika Anthony

Today's global business environment makes your job more complex and difficult, especially when it comes to issues of cultural adaptation. Managers must respond to nuances in communication styles, as well as deal with different expectations that employees have of their leaders across cultures. And not meeting those expectations may doom your chance for success.

Personnel Decisions International (PDI) surveyed nearly 250 companies—many of them members of the *Fortune* 500—and asked more than 3,600 bosses to rate 24 managerial competencies by level of importance. Consistently, bosses worldwide rated the ability to "drive for results" and "analyze issues" as the most critically important competencies in mid-level managers. Most bosses worldwide also consistently rated the following managerial competencies as extremely important: "act with integrity," "sound judgment" and "manage execution." But just how a manager gets results, wins respect and leads employees within these parameters varies tremendously among countries, cultures and individuals.

Bosses in Japan, for example, rated the importance of "championing change" considerably higher than managers from other cultures, according to the PDI data. This finding may be indicative of the collectivistic culture of Japan, where communication tends to be more subtle and indirect. Managers often use consensus-building techniques to internalize change within the individual before anything is executed or acted upon. This cultural environment is ripe for conflict with the authoritative, do-it-now leadership style so common to Western management, as a *Fortune* 500 retailer discovered. Upper management became frustrated when its Japan operation delayed implementation of a new computerized system. Yet when the unit finally implemented the system, the effort was overwhelmingly more effective than the average 65 percent success rate the retailer achieved elsewhere. U.S. management learned that although the Japan operation was slow to "pull the trigger," it was striving to internalize ownership of the project before executing it. The result was a quick and well-executed change. It should come as no surprise that bosses in Japan rated the importance of "establishing plans" and "providing direction" among the top five managerial competencies.

In Latin America, previous research suggests that cultural behavior is commonly steeped in being specifically directed what to do. Here, the high "power distance" seen in some enterprises can stem from a hierarchical reporting structure and autocratic leadership style. In Latin cultures, inquiries into personal lives are often expected before business is transacted. Typically, it's assumed that business relationships will be built over time, based on trust. Notably, PDI's research showed that bosses in Mexico rated "act with integrity" as the most important managerial competency, followed by "drive for results" and "sound judgment."

In mainland China, what's known as micromanaging in the United States is more common and acceptable. Generally speaking, direct reports expect specific directions and detailed explanations from their managers, not broad goals. Previous research on culture has demonstrated that China's culture could be considered more risk-averse due to the social ramifications of failure. Failing can mean losing face in front of your employees, clients, leadership or society, a fate that many Chinese consider shameful. Likewise, managers in China often are seen as highly respected pillars of authority to which employees traditionally assign parental-like attributes. It's not uncommon for workers in China to seek personal advice from their supervisors, and white-collar workers might expect to be coached by their bosses. Bosses in China rated the importance of "fostering teamwork" higher than bosses in most other countries—as a top-five managerial competency.

In the Middle East, business has a strong social component, and personal and face-to-face communications are highly valued. Similar to Asian cultures, less emphasis is given to winning immediate results in this consensus-driven and nonconfrontational culture. Networks take on heightened importance to take care of business in the Middle East. Instead of bulldozing their way to get results, managers must engage elders—who may not necessarily be the highest-level executives of the organization but who wield informal influence and power.

In the midst of day-to-day business, getting perspective on these organizational-cultural issues is difficult at best. Nevertheless, managing within a different culture is really only an extension of what managers do every day—working with differences. When managers fail to adapt and respond to these differences, projects may fail and employees may clash. As these scenarios of cultural differences illustrate, managers need to delve outside their comfort zones, get to know the people they're working with and challenge their prejudgments.

Understanding Culture's Impact on Work Style

If you're managing employees from . . .	They may...
Japan	• Communicate in relatively subtle and indirect ways. • Want to achieve consensus before agreeing to execute a change initiative.
Latin America	• Want you to inquire into their personal lives before you bring up important work issues. • Assume that working relationships are built over time, based on trust.
Mainland China	• Look to you for specific directions and detailed explanations, rather than broad goals. • Seek personal advice from you.
The Middle East	• Emphasis consensus and harmony over confrontation and winning immediate results. • Look to sources of informal influence to get information and make decisions.

Watch Out for the Minefield of Hidden Bias
By Pamela Babcock

Mounting evidence says most people are more prejudiced than they think. The Implicit Association Test (IAT), a web-based series of exercises developed by a Harvard University research team, discovered a significant degree of implicit bias among those tested—despite what researchers say were honest assertions by test takers that they harbored no prejudices. The IAT was developed as part of a project designed to detect bias based on several factors, including race, gender, sexual orientation and national origin.

Researchers found that the highest levels of bias—70 percent or more—were directed at blacks, the elderly, the disabled, the overweight and other stigmatized groups. Furthermore, minorities internalized the same biases as majority groups. Researcher Tony Greenwald, a University of Washington psychology professor, was one of the first to take the test—and was immediately struck by the results. "We were initially surprised to find these biases in ourselves," says Greenwald. "After finding them in ourselves, we were not so surprised to find them in others."

As you know, bias—hidden or overt—can affect decisions as to who is hired and how you evaluate, promote and pay employees. Says Milton Perkins, SPHR, North Central regional director for the Society for Human Resource Management (SHRM) and staff leader of SHRM's Workplace Diversity Special Expertise Panel, hidden bias "will affect turnover and, at the end of the day, people who are hurting inside will inevitably hurt someone else; they will hurt your business, impact your customers and drain your productivity."

The good news? Individuals with an implicit bias don't always act in biased ways, says Greenwald. "We believe that people aware of their implicit biases can, if they wish, choose to suppress their expression by paying attention to their behavior in situations that allow possible discrimination," he says. "However, most people remain unaware of their implicit biases."

The key, then, is to start by recognizing these skewed perceptions. Greenwald says getting people to take one or more of the IAT exercises is "a first step" in building individual awareness of unconscious prejudices. Paul Steven Miller, a law professor at the University of Washington and former commissioner with the Equal Employment Opportunity Commission, agrees the test may be helpful in challenging people in a nonjudgmental way to think about biases they may harbor. "In fact, when someone is accused of discrimination, often people take great offense because it's an ugly accusation," Miller says. "And yet those same people, when you dive in and peel back the layers, may have biases ingrained that are affecting the decisions they make, the assignments they give and the promotion or hiring they do."

The test certainly had a surprising effect on staff members of the Montgomery, Ala.-based Southern Poverty Law Center (SPLC), a nonprofit organization dedicated to protecting civil rights and promoting tolerance, which was so interested in the IAT research that from 2001 to 2003 it provided funding to develop several tests. As a result, one might expect that center staff members would be more bias-free than other groups—yet the test revealed that they, too, had hidden biases.

"Bigotry is a persistent social problem in this country, and we can't escape being socialized in this context," says Jennifer Smith-Holladay, the center's senior adviser for strategic affairs. Smith-Holladay says her own results uncovered a preference for white people—a group to which she belongs— and a preference for "straight" people, a group to which she doesn't belong.

"I discovered that I not only have some in-group favoritism lurking in my subconscious, but also possess some internalized oppression in terms of my sexuality," she adds. Lesson learned? "In the case of my own subconscious in-group favoritism for white people, for example, my charge is to be color-conscious, not color-blind, and to always explicitly consider how race may affect behaviors and decisions."

Quinetta M. Roberson, associate professor of human resource studies at the Cornell University School of Industrial and Labor Relations, encourages managers to look at language used in various contexts—staffing, performance reviews and the identification of high-potential employees and succession planning or leadership candidates. The most obvious examples of loaded language involve using words to describe expectations about how people will behave, rather than their actual behavior, says Roberson; or using adjectives in a performance review to describe the employee, rather than simply stating what the employee's performance was, or whether that level of performance was acceptable. "Joe Smith is lazy" is a much different assessment from "Joe Smith did not complete a single task on time, thereby failing to meet his goals."

A more subtle case might relate to the verbs managers choose to describe employee performance. For example, writing that Joe Smith "exhibited good teamwork skills" suggests that although Joe has demonstrated these skills in the past, he may not necessarily be expected to do so in the future. Writing that Joe "is a great team player" is a broader statement about Joe, not just his demonstrated behavior, and implies that he may be expected to be a team player in the future.

Even if you don't take the IAT, here are some ways to combat bias:

- Use multiple interviewers with diverse backgrounds and different perspectives. This helps ensure that more valid and legally defensible hiring decisions are made—and that the impact of any biases held by individuals or groups is minimized.

- Use structured, rather than unstructured, interviews, in which all candidates are asked the same questions regardless of demographic characteristics or appearance. Unstructured interviews accurately predict on-the-job performance only 20 percent of the time, while structured interviews do somewhat better, at 50 percent.

- Set up a blind applicant-review system. A 2004 study of job candidates with white- and black-sounding names by the University of Chicago Graduate School of Business found uniform discrimination across occupations and industries. Federal contractors and employers claiming to be equal opportunity employers discriminated as much as other employers. As a way to counter this bias, employment lawyers recommend masking the names and addresses of applicants before circulating résumés.

Did You Know?

- By 2008, 41 percent of the United States' 39 million workers are projected to be members of minority groups.

- Hispanics make up the United States' fastest-growing minority.

- By 2050, minorities are expected to rise from one-fourth to one-half of the U.S. population.

- In the 2000 Census, nearly one in five U.S. residents reported speaking a foreign language regularly at home.

Showing Good Faith toward Muslim Employees
By Marc Adams

Although a recent study shows that nearly two-thirds of Muslim respondents felt very comfortable at their workplaces, Muslims' struggle for acceptance on the job increasingly is framed in terms of employee complaints. At the Equal Employment Opportunity Commission, Muslims' share of total religious discrimination complaints rose from 12 percent in 1992 to 15.5 percent in 1999. Those figures don't count other complaints that never get as far as the EEOC but that, instead, are mediated by Muslim groups.

According to a 1999 survey conducted by the Tanenbaum Center for Interreligious Understanding, based in New York, 76.5 percent of Muslim respondents were at least somewhat troubled by religious bias at work—the highest rate of concern for any of the religious groups surveyed, including Buddhists, Hindus or Jews. And 27 percent of Muslims said they had run into discrimination personally or knew other Muslims who had—second only to Hindus at 32 percent. Experts say the study demonstrates that employers still are coming to grips with religious accommodation and that acceptance of Muslims' strict religious code is an important test of employers' commitment to diversity.

The challenge for many managers is how to accommodate Islamic religious practices that may seem out of place at work. Under Title VII of the 1964 Civil Rights Act, religious accommodation isn't optional. The law requires employers to accommodate sincerely held religious beliefs unless the accommodation poses "undue hardship," which generally is measured by the arrangement's cost. For example, suppose you have to hire a temporary worker to replace an employee who is absent for religious reasons. If you're paying top dollar for the temp and you have to do it often, you can probably claim undue hardship.

In most cases, however, managers can accommodate Islamic requirements in a variety of ways, as shown in the following examples.

Prayer: Muslims must pray five times a day between dawn and late evening. For most employees, two or three prayer times probably will fall during working hours, depending on their shifts. These prayers are brief, usually only a few minutes long; some Muslims say the daily prayers take less time than many employees' coffee breaks or smoking breaks. Privacy isn't required, but workers can't be interrupted during prayer. Employees also must attend Friday prayer services that take place around midday and last between 45 and 90 minutes.

For daily prayer obligations, managers can:

- Offer "floating" breaks that any worker can use for any reason, including prayer.

- Require employees to use leave time for daily prayer or weekly services.

- Require workers to make up time taken for prayer.

- Provide separate rooms that anyone can use for any reason, including prayer. No religious group is entitled to exclusive treatment.

To accommodate employees' weekly group prayers on Fridays, employers can permit an extended lunch hour.

Appearance: Some Muslim men wear beards and kufis, or skull caps; some women wear hijabs, which are scarves that cover the head or the entire body, as a sign of modesty. Safety regulations still apply when an employee asks for a religious accommodation for dress or facial hair. Some employers require bearded men to wear hair nets or masks for health or safety reasons. Hijabs can be adjusted for safety reasons or even tailored to match the employer's uniforms. One fast-food chain provided employees with hijabs in its distinctive company colors.

Ramadan: During this month-long observance of discipline and prayer, Muslims must fast until sunset. Workers on some shifts—say, noon to 8 p.m.—might have to adjust their meal breaks accordingly. The timing of Ramadan is based on the lunar calendar; for managers, the key thing to remember is that Ramadan's dates move slightly each year, with the holy month generally beginning about 10 days earlier each year.

Holidays: The major Islamic holidays are Eid ul-Fitr and Eid ul-Adha. Eid ul-Fitr marks the end of the Ramadan fast. It's a three-day holiday, but most employees take time off only on the first day after Ramadan ends. Eid ul-Adha marks the end of the annual pilgrimage to Mecca and occurs on the 10th day of the 12th Islamic month. That's around Dec. 31 in 2006. Employees can use vacation time or personal days for these holidays. Some companies provide "floating" holidays that any employee can use for any purpose. You can require Muslim workers to give adequate notice if they want to take holidays off.

Aim for Quality Relationships to Keep Young, Diverse Workers
By Catherine Dixon-Kheir

If you're losing young and culturally diverse talent to greener pastures, you probably don't know why. Departing employees may have cited higher salaries, bigger stock options or a promotion as reasons for leaving; but more than likely they didn't believe they had a quality relationship with their managers.

These relationships are particularly important in retaining employees in the age group of 21 to 30, as well as those from culturally diverse backgrounds, such as black, Latino/Hispanic, Asian/Pacific Islander or Native American, according to surveys by Alignment Strategies Inc. Those who left felt isolated, excluded from formal and informal communication channels and networks and without mentors or sponsors. But to avoid "burning bridges" or leaving a negative impression, most cited better salaries or better opportunities as reasons for leaving.

"The talented employee may join a company ... but how long that employee stays and how productive he is while he is there is determined by his relationship with his immediate supervisor," say Marcus Buckingham and Curt Coffman in a study that analyzed 25 years of Gallup interviews with more than 1 million employees in a broad range of companies and countries (*First, Break All The Rules: What The World's Greatest Managers Do Differently*, Simon & Schuster, 1999).

The supervisory relationship not only influences job performance, career development, recognition and rewards, it also extends to such matters as teamwork, communication, organizational resources, even relationships with co-workers, customers and other managers. But managers and employees interact most frequently about work transactions and often lack the time—or believe it's inappropriate—to get to know each other's needs, motivations and personal goals. This thinking often makes the relationship superficial; communication is based on a "need to know basis" rather than on a more authentic level where straight talk could include "the bad news with the good news."

To discover how successful supervisors are addressing these challenges, Alignment Strategies interviewed 500 managers from a cross section of industries identified by employees as having established and sustained quality reporting relationships with younger employees and those from culturally diverse groups. These supervisors were found to engage in similar practices. Generally, they:

- Set mutual expectations.

- Provided frequent feedback.

- Avoided generalities or stereotypes in communicating.

- Shared personal experiences and cultural knowledge of the organization.

- Acted as an advocate and provided visibility and exposure for employees.

- Were accessible and encouraged "straight talk about the bad news as well as the good news."

- Knew and appreciated the employee's work.

- Coached and developed knowledge and skills.

- Recognized and rewarded superior performance.

Of the respondents to the survey, 80 percent said the quality of communication was more important than its frequency. Most of the supervisors focused the relationship on job performance but emphasized that they spent time getting to know the values and personal interests of their workers. They reported that trust was higher when they connected with their subordinates personally as well as professionally.

Alignment Strategies also surveyed 500 employees between the ages of 21 and 30; 75 percent were from minority groups. All were asked to identify their key requirements for having long careers with their organizations. Overwhelmingly, a quality supervisory relationship was listed as a top factor. They said the attributes of a quality supervisory relationship included the following:

- Effective introduction to the organization, such as introductions to co-workers and other managers with whom they would come in contact, as well as information on the organization's culture and "unwritten rules."

- Recognition and support for career aspirations and contributions.

- Facilitation of acceptance and inclusion in the organization and in professional groups and informal networks.

- Advancement of their ideas and proposals to benefit the organizations.

- Support in difficult situations and going to bat on their behalf in battles they cannot win on their own.

To improve the quality of your relationships with your subordinates, take some—or all—of the following steps:

Learn more about your employees. Compare viewpoints on such matters as job expectations, what they believe they do best, their overall sense of inclusion and the resources, tools and materials needed for them to be effective.

Find out what it takes to make them happy at work. Ask each of your direct reports what it will take to keep them with your organization, and use this information to create action plans to retain valuable talent.

Set mutual expectations about the supervisory relationship. Discuss the behaviors that help and hinder a quality reporting relationship, and identify specific actions necessary to achieve the relationship you both want. Then, set a schedule to discuss progress on the relationship. This sets the tone for open communication and eliminates misguided assumptions about what is important in a quality relationship.

Schedule regular discussions about career and/or personal development goals. Encourage your employees to discuss their goals with you, and establish realistic development plans to support them. Cover topics such as assignments, visibility, mentors, line management support, timing and scheduled follow-up dates.

Give regular feedback. Use discussions about mistakes, errors or failures as a learning opportunity, and coach your employees on how to handle similar situations in the future. This builds trust in two ways: Employees are realistic about how their managers view their performance, and you eliminate "surprises" during formal performance reviews.

Encourage dialogue about diversity. Let your employees know that your workplace values differences and that they can discuss different perspectives and cultural viewpoints with you. Share some experiences in which you demonstrate the value of diversity and provide examples of how diversity helps build the organization.

Look for opportunities to support relationship building among others. Seek situations in which your employees can meet others who support their goals. This can be as simple as including them in conference calls, meetings and lunches or having them sit in on one of your meetings.

Quick Tips for Managing Diversity

- Do you struggle to lead a culturally diverse team? Recognize the role that each employee's culture plays on his or her work; for example, feelings about group versus individual achievement, treatment of schedules and deadlines, communication style and approach to conflict resolution. Avoid interpreting an employee's behavior through the prism of your own cultural background. And search for alternate management approaches that are more compatible with an employee's cultural background.

- Want to know what employees from different cultures expect from you? Educate yourself about how people from Japan, Latin America, China, the Middle East and elsewhere view authority figures, make decisions, build working relationships and implement change.

- Do many of your employees speak primary languages other than English? Practice "mutual accommodation" by clarifying what languages are to be spoken during which hours at work and when employees may speak their native tongue. Avoid illegal demands for English-speaking only—such as prohibiting use of another language during work breaks.

- Think you aren't prejudiced? Most people have hidden biases toward stigmatized groups—particularly blacks, the elderly, the disabled and the overweight. Honestly recognize your own biases. Then combat them by considering how they influence your decisions regarding hiring, retention and employee development and promotion.

- Are some of your employees Muslim? Many Muslims experience religious bias at work. To avoid charges of religious discrimination, familiarize yourself with Islam's religious code. Accommodate Islamic practices (such as daily prayer and Muslim dress) as long as doing so doesn't cause undue hardship, incur unreasonable cost or compromise on-the-job safety.

- Losing young and culturally diverse talent to greener pastures? Improve the quality of your supervisory relationship with these employees—including finding out what makes them happy at work, regularly discussing their career aspirations and encouraging dialogue about diversity.

SECTION THREE:
MOTIVATING WORKERS TO EXCEL

Hiring and managing diverse, talented employees won't mean much to your organization's performance unless your people feel motivated to give their best on the job. Indeed, inspiring your people to excel counts among the most crucial tasks of a manager.

This section provides you with powerful techniques and tools for unleashing your direct reports' desire to reach their highest potential. Ideas include challenging your people with ambitious expectations, showing your appreciation and respect for what your subordinates bring to the table, and promoting confidence and job satisfaction among your employees.

Practice the Five R's to Motivate Workers
By R. Brayton Bowen

Compensation pundits frequently suggest that the "right" reward system will drive performance by motivating workers to achieve new levels of performance. But rewards alone don't drive organizational behavior. In an age where loyalty is dead and at-will employment reigns, free agent workers are looking for currency that involves more than just pay. That's why successful managers are exchanging the old reward system for "new age currency," one minted in the five denominations of responsibility, respect, relationships, recognition and rewards. And, while it may not look like greenbacks, pesos or euros, rest assured you can bank on the results.

Responsibility

Few jobs are designed with a specific employee in mind. Job descriptions are more like extensive to-do lists with a catch-all phrase at the end, such as "... and other tasks as directed by management." The underlying message is, "Do whatever I tell you," which shifts the responsibility of the job to the manager, not the employee. By creating a job description with your employees that profiles the work processes and desired outcomes, you empower your employees by assigning them accountability and responsibility. For example, Henry Ford was known for his straightforward approach to partnering with employees in designing jobs. He reportedly would take a difficult production job to the "laziest" (substitute "most resourceful") worker on the line to see how many shortcuts would be taken. To be sure, workers involved in this way felt valued and took full ownership for the production process once it hit their stations.

To encourage responsibility, take the following steps:

- Work with your HR department to see that jobs are properly profiled for your people and stated outcomes are relevant to the business. Done well, the profile should serve as a template for planning and managing performance, as well as a report card for review purposes.

- Talk regularly to your employees about ways to increase alignment between what they do and where the company is headed.

- Eliminate tasks and activities that are unessential to your primary mission.

- Continuously seek out ways to add value.

Respect

Jeffrey Pfeffer, Ph.D., a professor at the Stanford Graduate School of Business, maintains that organizations with "pro-people practices" tend to perform up to 40 percent better over time. Such organizations include Southwest Airlines, Men's Wearhouse and Toyota Motor Manufacturing. "Respectful" organizations build cultures of continuous learning, teamwork and genuine caring and concern for all key stakeholders—employees, customers, communities, suppliers and investors.

In these kinds of organizations, performance review systems are aimed at building confidence and competence, unlike other systems seemingly designed to restrict pay increases and root out some percentage of the workforce regardless of their value.

Information—the lifeblood of every knowledgeable organization—flows freely throughout the system, as people are valued and respected for the intellectual capital they contribute. And, prudent risk-taking is encouraged in the interest of building excellent organizations. Managers attend to and show they value feelings, ideas and actions. People are appreciated not only for what they know and do but also for the emotional intelligence they bring to the organization.

Even if your organization isn't into "pro-people" practices, you can follow that model with the people you lead, with the following tips:

- When preparing performance reviews, take time to educate and communicate as well as evaluate, and identify ways to succeed.

- Use language that is constructive and prescriptive. And be sure to liberally add "please" and "thank you" to your vocabulary as a courtesy extended to employees and customers alike.

- Engage your people in developing "operating principles" or a "vision" that expresses how everyone will work with one another and with employees throughout the system, how customers are to be served and how communications are to flow.

- Build on the concept of teamwork—respecting differences, solving problems collaboratively, supporting one another and performing as a team.

- Avoid negative energy, such as gossiping, harassing, triangulating relationships, etc.

- Focus on positive energy by setting norms and performing beyond expectations.

Relationships

If you recall your childhood school days and some of the styles of your teachers, you'll probably remember what was productive and counterproductive in motivating you. The strict disciplinarian who taught by fear and intimidation never focused on the "joy of learning." On the other hand, if you had a teacher who used a constructive strategy that focused all attention on the process of discovery and personal development, you learned to think for yourself and to strive continuously for rewards of enlightenment and mastery. Similarly, the strategy of the effective manager is one of facilitation and education.

Because motivation is an inside job—something individuals choose to unleash under the right circumstances—the effective manager must focus on creating environments that are conducive to workers getting motivated. Coaching, teaching, supporting and guiding—all are strategies that have the best chance of producing the right outcomes. And above all, being authentic, honest and ethical is absolutely critical. Indeed, the No. 1 attribute of leaders most valued by employees is honesty. Without trust, employees will not take risk, get motivated or run the gauntlet.

Recognition

Recognition has more to do with being appreciated than getting credit, but too many organizations waste valuable time, energy and resources on gestures of questionable value, such as parking spaces for employees of the month or tickets for two at an upscale restaurant. A better motivator is recognition that comes in the form of assignments to join a special project, lead a study team or scope out a new system.

Of course, recognition also comes in the form of promotions and public accolades. In organizations where the emphasis is on achieving as a team, internal politics and aggressive competition are appropriately low, while crediting others with a job well done is the standard. For any number of employees, particularly in entry-level and minimum-wage positions, the psychic income of being openly and regularly appreciated goes a long way toward enhancing worker retention and commitment.

Rewards

While rewards are important, they are fifth in importance with respect to the five R's. If people are paid fairly and competitively and they are informed as to how the system works, pay is a "satisfier," to quote Frederick Herzberg, but not a motivator. To provide optimum return on investment, rewards must be an integral part of an overall recognition and reward strategy—linking business goals and objectives with the other four R's.

Beginning with job profiles, rewards must be aligned to compensable factors centering on responsibility, such as "satisfying customers," "building quality products" and, as an example for managers, "increasing workforce competence." Outcomes such as these can be quantified, and managers and employees can mutually agree on goals. By identifying the right goals, attributes and competencies for your people, you can be a resource for HR because when it comes to the work and what it takes to be successful, you're the expert.

Other reward elements, such as employee stock ownership plans, 401(k)s and the like, should be clearly linked to company performance. You can help here by providing important operational and financial objectives for your area. Moreover, such dimensions as respect can be measured and compensable in terms of building self-esteem, enhancing company reputation, exemplifying company values, etc. Effective relationships can be equated to teamwork, strategic leadership (for managers), and customer relations. And both intrinsic and extrinsic rewards can then be awarded and allocated for recognition purposes.

How Motivating Are You?

For each statement below, check whether you agree or disagree.

To motivate my employees, I...	Agree	Disagree
1. Make sure job descriptions profile work processes and desired outcomes relevant to our business.	❑	❑
2. Genuinely value the knowledge and skills my people bring to the table.	❑	❑
3. Take time to help my people constantly strengthen their personal and professional abilities.	❑	❑
4. Let my subordinates know that I appreciate them.	❑	❑
5. Link rewards to measurable business results.	❑	❑

The more you checked "Agree," the more likely you effectively motivate your workers to excel. Where you checked "Disagree," consider how you might strengthen your skill in that aspect.

You Don't Need Cash to Show Appreciation to Your Employees
By Charlotte Garvey

Getting a mug with the company logo on it probably isn't enough to stop an unhappy employee from quitting. But experts agree that small tokens of recognition presented with the right message and style can make employees feel appreciated—and underscore a company's values.

"Really powerful recognition has to do with the feeling and energy behind it, not the cost," says Alan G. Robinson, co-author of *Ideas Are Free* (Berrett-Koehler Publishers, 2004), a book highlighting successful businesses that use nonmonetary recognition to reward employees who come up with innovative ideas.

For example, at a Toyota plant in India that Robinson visited, walls and machinery were "festooned with stickers" to indicate where employees had suggested innovative ideas, The stickers were cheap, distinctive and included the name of the suggester on each one. Those stickers served as their own reward for employees, Robinson says, because employees could walk by the visual reminders, point and say, "That's my idea."

Employees crave recognition like that, says Bob Nelson, president of San Diego-based Nelson Motivation Inc., and author of several best-selling rewards and recognition books. In a survey he conducted assessing the employee recognition practices most valued by 750 employees across various industries, Nelson found that those ranked at the top involved no cost at all. The No. 1 most important recognition from a manager?

Support and involvement, followed by personal praise and autonomy and authority. Cash and other monetary awards came in at No. 10.

At T. Rowe Price, the Spotlight on Excellence program emphasizes the company's values, says Cathy Plakatoris, vice president for recruiting, retention and development at the Baltimore-based financial services company. In addition to a spontaneous, on-the-spot program for a specific achievement, which includes handwritten and electronic thank-you messages, T. Rowe Price uses a more formal recognition program to focus on employees who in the long run do work that embodies principles that the company wants to emphasize. Peers or managers are encouraged to nominate employees whose work demonstrates teamwork, service, leadership, integrity or initiative.

For some companies and managers, recognition also is about employee visibility. Employers and managers hope that employees who see someone getting kudos will aspire to achieve similarly so they, too, can be recognized. But the personal touch remains a key factor in how recognition is perceived by employees. Experts suggest that managers or peers carefully consider the way in which each employee would appreciate being recognized.

"As a rule of thumb, public recognition is desired by most employees—but not all," says Nelson. "It would be wrong to give an employee public recognition when he didn't want that and was embarrassed by it." A manager who knows his employees well should have a handle on how to recognize them in a way that is appreciated by each individual, whether it be in a meeting with a client, in a hallway among co-workers or privately.

One mistake companies make with recognition programs is creating a one-size-fits-all solution that aspires to the lowest common denominator. A personal, individual touch, on the other hand, can go a long way. "One quick thank-you note on your manager's stationery is worth a whole lot more than a cup and a T-shirt with a form letter," says Robinson.

Raise Expectations on Productivity—and Watch Your Workers Exceed Them
By Thomas K. Connellan

If you're looking for ways to bump productivity, rescue slumping performers or improve teamwork, start with your expectations. These subtle—but very powerful—elements of your leadership tool kit can produce lasting results.

Raising your expectations doesn't require you to adopt a perpetual cheery optimism, but it does require you to make a brutally realistic assessment of current conditions. If productivity is low, cycle time is horrible and/or quality is poor, you need to acknowledge the facts—or you'll never be able to improve performance. And part of that brutal assessment requires looking in the mirror. Perhaps, without realizing it, your underlying beliefs are contributing to the performance situations you see around you.

Three components make up the messages you send: the words you use, the way you say them and your non-verbal cues.

Words

Here are some examples of how to frame your expectations for performance improvement in three different situations.

- If productivity is down, you might say: "Well, as we look at productivity, we can see that it's 2 percent below where it was last year. I know we can get back to where we were—and eventually beyond—because we have the horsepower right in this room to do it." In selecting these words, you've acknowledged where performance is and expressed confidence about improvement.

- If you're making progress in an area—but more progress is required—the message might be: "While we're making progress on quality, it's still not where it needs to be. I know we can get to where we need to be by continuing our Six Sigma efforts. Let's look and see where we need to put our resources next."

- If performance is good and you want to boost it more, the message should be: "Cycle time is good, never been better. Let's look at how to cut it even further. I know we can do it if we work together to figure out how."

In each example, your words describe the present situation in simple and direct terms and also express confidence in moving to further improvement.

Verbal Intonations

The tone of your voice is the second element of your message. Everyone has experienced situations where the words sent one message and the tone of voice sent another. When there's a conflict, most people believe what is conveyed by the tone of your voice. So, make sure that your tone matches the positive message of your words. Not only should you avoid the obvious mismatch, but also the unintentional mismatch—those occasional situations where your words say one thing and your tone of voice says another.

Nonverbal Cues

The bulk of the meaning lies here. You can say the words, and your tone of voice can match the words. But if you're looking around, tapping your fingers, shaking your head "no" or doing any one of the hundreds of other seemingly little things that say, "I don't believe in you," you're not going to get the performance you want. Here are five categories to check yourself against:

1. **Body position.** If your arms are crossed, your legs are crossed away from the person you're communicating with or you're giving the "cold shoulder," then you're sending negative messages. On the other hand, if your body position is open—you're facing the person rather than looking away—you communicate honesty, warmth and openness. If your posture is erect rather than slumping, you communicate positive beliefs. And if you're leaning slightly forward, you demonstrate interest in the other individual.

2. **Hand gestures.** Avoid tapping your fingers ("I'm impatient"), hiding your mouth ("I'm hiding something"), wagging your finger (the equivalent of poking someone with your finger) and closed or clenched hands ("I'm upset"). These gestures all conflict with an "I believe in you" message. Instead, use open hands with palms up ("I'm being honest with nothing to hide") or touching your hands to your chest ("I believe in what I'm saying"). Both of these emphasize a positive message.

3. **Head.** If your head is shaking back and forth or tilted off to one side, you're sending a message of disbelief. On the other hand, if your head is facing directly toward someone and you're nodding up and down, you're delivering a nonverbal message of belief and confidence.

4. **Facial expressions.** Smile, and keep your mouth relaxed. Show alertness in your face and act like you're ready to listen. Do these regularly and you'll have created an open communication pattern with someone who will believe in your sincerity. On the other hand, if you're tight-lipped, are clenching your jaw muscles and have only a grim smile, no smile at all or a frown, you'll send a message that says: "No way can you possibly succeed at this project."

5. **Eyes.** Maintaining good eye contact is one of the most important nonverbal signals you can send. It conveys the message, "I'm interested in you and when I say I believe in you, I really do." Making sure that your eyes are open wide is also helpful. Squinting can deter the recipient. Worse yet is looking around, paying attention to other things and not paying attention to the person or topic at hand.

Communicate high expectations well enough and you may even have to step aside to avoid getting run over by a team of committed players whose performance is accelerating.

Turn Your Disengaged Workers into "Bright-Eyed" Contributors
By Eric Allenbaugh

Three company cultures generally emerge in corporate America—and you can often identify the presence of a particular culture by looking into the eyes of employees. While all three employee groups often exist within a given company, a dominant group defines the overall culture. Here is what you will likely see—and experience:

The 'Glazed Eye' Group. About 54 percent of employees fall into this category, a group characterized by lack of spirit and vitality. They're quick to explain why something cannot be done and frequently offer excuses. They look to others to fix problems and seldom share creative ideas. They feel discounted, unappreciated and insignificant. They're likely to make statements such as "Nobody listens to me," "It's not my job" and "They don't care."

Members of this group avoid risk-taking at almost all cost, do the absolute minimum they can to get by and tend to watch the clock very closely. They range between neutral and mildly negative about the company, yet don't feel motivated to do anything to improve the situation. When this group dominates, it will slowly drain the vitality out of an organization.

The 'Beady Eye' Group. Members of this actively disengaged group represent about 17 percent of the corporate workforce, but dealing with their negative energy often consumes a disproportionate amount of time, talent and treasure. These people work against the organization and go out of their way to seek out and find the flaws—and they do find them.

They focus on problems and resist attempts to deal with solutions. They feel angry, frustrated and highly disconnected. Blaming, moaning and whining, you will likely hear them say things like "My boss is a jerk," "This place is the pits," "The pay and benefits are lousy" and "This is hopeless."

Although these employees do not like working in this environment, they tend to resist efforts to improve working relationships. Many get their power through open resistance and cynicism. Even though they may be relatively small in number, their relentless negative energy drags others down. Their high stress levels contribute to the stress of others. In some respects, they take some degree of pleasure when a leader fails or even when the organization fails.

The 'Bright Eye' Group. This "dream team" represents about 29 percent of the employee population in corporate America. Bright eye employees are highly engaged and committed to the mission, vision and values of the organization. A "can-do" attitude characterizes their behavior, they go the extra mile in giving and doing their best and they function in a spirit of partnership with other employees and with their customers. These people have a clear understanding of personal accountability and tend to look to themselves first for resources and solutions. Instead of fixing blame, they fix the problems.

Bright eye employees embrace change and look for ways to reinvent themselves while continuing to provide high value. They work hard, yet seem to be energized by the quality and significance of their work. They take great pride in their accomplishments and speak well of their company. You will likely hear such statements from them as "I love my job," "This is a great place to work," "This feels like home to me" and "I am proud to work here."

So, how do you go about creating and sustaining a bright eye culture? It's not rocket science; you just need to stick to the basics—but do them exceptionally well. Here are six strategies for taking talent to the top:

1. **Hire winners.** Take the time to hire well. Southwest Airlines "hires for attitude and trains for skill," and its long-term results reflect this commitment. When evaluating potential employees, consider the three A's to ensure long-term success:

- Attitude: Do they have the right spirit for this job?

- Aptitude: Do they have the right talent for this job?

- Alignment: Are they the right fit with our mission and values?

2. **Engage their spirit.** To motivate others:

- Find out what turns people on about their jobs and do more of that.

- Find out what turns people off about their jobs and do less of that.

It's amazing what happens when you actually talk with and listen to your employees about what's important to them, as well as following through with assignments that engage their spirit.

3. **Coach for success.** Coaching is an ongoing, collaborative process intended to clarify performance targets, reinforce strengths and encourage individuals to stretch to even higher levels of performance. Building ongoing coaching into the culture produces a high return on the investment while engaging people in their own success and effectiveness.

4. **Focus on deliverables.** A meaningful mission and challenging goals tend to bring out the creative best in others. People want to do a good job, they want to contribute, they want to make a difference, and they want to have pride in their work. Your job is to make sure people are aligned with and enthusiastic about a meaningful purpose—and to

engage their spirit in exceeding expected results. Celebrate successes and look for the learning when mistakes are made.

5. **Clear their path.** Like the conductor of an orchestra, your job is to "bring out their music" by encouraging employees' individual and synergistic best. You don't play their instruments. You engage their spirit to release the music within. As a leader, a coach and a facilitator, your primary job is to provide them with the resources they need, remove the barriers, make the connections and encourage their individual and collective best. In short, create the environment for them to excel and get out of their way.

6. **Commit to renewal.** Maintaining the status quo in a competitive environment is not a viable option. If your team merely stayed at its current state of development for the next several years, it might become an "endangered species." Ask yourself: "Are we lagging behind in our field, are we just keeping up, or are we one of the progressive leaders?" Even if your team is moving ahead, the speed at which it is moving must be faster than the speed at which global business advances. Otherwise, your team will still trail behind.

As most employees want to learn and grow on the job, consider the three R's of renewal: Release, reaffirm and reinvent. To stay at the cutting edge, ask yourself:

- What must the team release or let go of to provide room and resources to support growth?

- What existing strengths and resources does the team need to reaffirm and intensify to support its next growth steps?

- How might the team reinvent itself to ensure that it remains at the cutting edge in its field?

Did You Know ?

- About 54 percent of employees lack spirit, vitality and a willingness to take needed risks.

- About 17 percent of employees go out of their way to seek out and find flaws in their organizations.

- About 29 percent of employees are highly engaged and committed to their organizations' mission, vision and values.

Create an Environment Where Employees Choose to Be Accountable
By Keith Ayers

A lot of leadership development is focused on the qualities or characteristics required to be a great leader. All this does is focus leaders on themselves, often resulting in an egocentric approach. The emphasis should not be on leaders but on the environment they create.

In his best-selling book *Good to Great*, author Jim Collins says: "First, get the right people on the bus, the wrong people off the bus and the right people in the right seats." If you have the right people, then trust them, believe in them and partner with them to create a great company. If you have people who aren't performing, make sure that you have created an environment where they can perform or that they are not just in the wrong seats—before you get them off the bus. You really won't know whether you have the right people until you have given them the opportunity to show what they are capable of in a responsibility-based culture.

Many managers fear entrusting employees with the responsibility of defining their own success and determining how to reach it through their performance. As a result, managers attempt to hold people accountable by insisting on compliance with policies and procedures, establishing goals and performance standards for employees, or offering incentives in an attempt to motivate people to comply. The research does not support this fear. Employees who are trusted and given more say over how they do their jobs are more engaged, more committed and more productive. And, people who know that their managers trust them to be responsible do not want to disappoint their managers.

The primary fear employees have about being held accountable is that there will be negative consequences if they don't succeed, perhaps even the loss of their jobs. It is safer for them to avoid risk by doing just what they are told. Employees who will not accept responsibility do not trust management enough to take the risk. They need to know that they will get the support they need to do their best and that mistakes will be treated as learning experiences, rather than as opportunities for blame and punishment.

The foundation of a responsibility-based culture is a high level of trust. When trust between management and employees is high, the following occur:

- Information is exchanged freely, feelings and opinions are openly discussed and people do not harbor hidden agendas.

- Expectations are clear, disagreements are discussed and resolved and individual performance is discussed and agreed on without the need for a formal process.

- Differences are valued, employees feel respected for their contribution and have input into how the organization can be more successful.

- People keep their commitments, strive for excellence in everything they do and can count on each other for support.

The most important factor in building trust with employees is to understand that being trustworthy does not mean your employees will trust you. You have to earn it. There are four behaviors, called the "elements of trust," that must be present for trust to develop:

1. **Congruence.** People see you as congruent when they know that what you say is on track with what you believe and what you know to be true and is aligned with what you do. Sometimes managers attempt to

sugarcoat bad news, or they are so "gentle" that the real message is not fully communicated. But in the long run that approach doesn't work. Even if you are temporarily able to smooth over a rough situation or take the pain out of an unpleasant encounter, sooner or later it will catch up and trust will be diminished or destroyed.

2. **Openness.** People tend to cooperate with people who will level with them and give them the whole story, even though some of the details may be a bit unpleasant. If you discover a change of plans that affects other people or you are displeased with their work results, tell them first. If there has been a delivery delay, tell your clients first. They will respect and trust you more for your openness. You'll also be perceived as a straight-shooter, and people will want to perform for you.

3. **Acceptance.** All people want to be accepted for who they are, not judged, criticized or made to feel inferior. It isn't always easy for managers to do that. You're in your position because you're competent, know the company and know what can and can't be done. It's easy to give the impression to others that they are slightly stupid or inadequate for not understanding as much about the company, department or project as you do. Acceptance doesn't mean that you have to accept poor performance or unacceptable behavior, but there is a difference between judging a person for who he is and judging what he does.

4. **Reliability.** People want to know if you do what you say you will do. Don't make promises you can't keep, even if you think it will get the job done for you now or appease an angry situation. In the long run it will hurt you. Do what you say you will do, and if you can't or won't do it, don't say you will.

Create an Environment That Promotes Confidence, Trust, and Satisfaction to Motivate Employees
By Thad Green

Why should you care about motivating your employees? The bottom line: Managers pay a heavy price when employees have motivation problems. When high-performing employees have unresolved motivation issues, their performance either declines or they leave for another job. When poor-performing employees are not motivated to improve, they drag down results, reduce productivity among their team members and, worse, seldom leave because they have no place to go.

The crux of motivation management is to understand that employees are motivated by what they believe is going to happen, not by what managers promise will happen. Managers can motivate employees by setting in motion the three conditions required for motivation—confidence, trust and satisfaction—and by creating an environment that reinforces those conditions.

Confidence problems. When employees believe they "can't do it," they tend to give up. That attitude typically develops when performance expectations are unrealistic, workloads are impossibly high and training fails to keep pace with employee needs. The problem is that managers often fail to realize the seriousness of this problem because employees are afraid to tell the boss they "can't do it" for fear that the boss will assign the duty to someone else. So, employees go through the motions, giving the appearance that everything is fine. As a result, confidence problems go largely unnoticed.

Good managers learn to recognize when an employee says he can do something but doesn't mean it. For instance, if the employee responds to an assignment by saying, "If everything goes well, I'll probably be able to … I guess," then clearly the employee has a confidence issue. If the employee doesn't volunteer information, ask questions in a nonthreatening way about how he plans to carry out the instructions. To ferret out confidence issues, ask:

- Do you know what is expected?
- Do you think what's expected is attainable?
- Can you do what is being asked of you and can you do it on time?

Most importantly, managers can improve motivation by assigning work to employees that they naturally do well and that they enjoy.

Trust problems. Employees face a major motivational roadblock when they don't believe outcomes are tied to their performance. These problems tend to be easier for managers to spot because employees usually are vocal about them. If you're concerned about trust issues, ask the employee:

- Do you know what is being offered for good performance?
- In your opinion, have we come through on our promises in the past?
- Do you expect to get what is offered?
- What do you expect to get if you do a good job?
- What do you expect to happen if you perform poorly?

Trust problems cannot be corrected quickly, and it takes courage for managers to give employees what their performance deserves. It may be easy to reward the high performers, but it is sometimes uncomfortable to withhold rewards when people perform poorly. It is particularly difficult when the poor-performing employee is either an outspoken troublemaker or a loyal, dedicated and hard-working employee. But not giving employees what their performance deserves sends a crippling message to the underperforming employee—as well as his teammates who learn they don't have to perform to get what they want.

Managers also make the mistake of giving too much trust. Managers who delegate duties to employees and then never follow up may think they are doing the right thing by giving employees space and independence. But, in fact, they are not reinforcing positive behaviors or correcting negative behaviors. Employees want managers to follow up on assignments to find out what they are doing right and what they could do better. Tying positive outcomes to the employee's bonus reinforces those behaviors and improves productivity.

Satisfaction Problems. It is difficult for employees to put out the effort necessary to get their work done if they are dissatisfied. People may believe they can do the job (confidence) and that outcomes will be tied to performance (trust), but they will not be motivated if they believe the outcomes will be unsatisfactory. It does not make sense for anyone to work hard for something he doesn't want.

Many managers fail to take the time to find out what is satisfying and dissatisfying to each employee. When motivating employees, many managers make the mistake of believing and acting as though everyone is motivated in the same way. But motivations differ. For example, some employees are motivated by challenging work, while others find it intimidating. Some prefer the certainty of a fixed routine; others thrive on task variety.

Managers also cannot assume that each individual employee will be satisfied if the three "big outcomes"—money, advancement and job security—are fulfilled. Other outcomes, such as praise, recognition, openness or honesty may be more motivating to some employees.

The solution to this problem is simple: Ask your employees what outcomes motivate them. Employees will gladly tell you what they want from you. Another interesting point is that when the work itself is satisfying, employees tend to be very forgiving when there is a shortfall in rewards. Why? Because employees are getting something that is highly prized by most people in today's work environment—enjoyment from their work.

Quick Tips for Motivating Your Team

- Wondering if you're using all available tools to motivate direct reports? In addition to rewards, you need four additional "R's": responsibility (clearly defining desired outcomes that are relevant to your business), respect (expressing genuine caring and concern for employees), relationships (facilitating your people's personal and professional development) and recognition (showing your appreciation for the intellectual capital your people bring to the table).

- Need more ideas for recognizing employees' value? Use small tokens that underscore your company's values—such as displaying stickers describing innovative ideas and naming the employees who contributed them. Adapt your recognition to individual employee preferences (for example, private versus public accolades).

- Want to communicate your expectations for higher performance from your team? Acknowledge where current performance is and express your confidence that your people can improve. Make your tone and body language match your words' positive message. For example, use an upbeat tone while also nodding as you lay out your vision of even better performance.

- Seeking to increase the percentage of "bright eyed" (highly engaged and committed) workers in your group? Give people assignments that engage their enthusiasm. Clarify their performance targets. Provide them with the resources they need to excel. And help them make the changes needed to stay at the top of their game.

- Want to cultivate trust, so your people take responsibility for improving their performance? Practice these four behaviors: congruence (ensuring that what you say reflects what you believe), openness (telling people the whole story, even if the details are unpleasant), acceptance (avoiding judging people for who they are) and reliability (doing what you say you'll do).

- Wondering what else—besides trust—are keys to motivating high performance? Consider confidence and job satisfaction. When employees believe they "can do it," they generally can. And when they're satisfied with their job conditions (including the level of variety in their work and the degree of challenge), they tend to perform better.

SECTION FOUR:
STRENGTHENING YOUR PEOPLE'S SKILLS

In today's business world, the most valuable employees look for organizations that will help them develop their talents. By strengthening your people's skills, you not only improve their productivity, you also retain your best performers and free up more of your own time by being able to delegate more to them.

The articles in this section contain useful suggestions for sharpening your employees' abilities. You'll find advice ranging from how to ensure that your subordinates retain what they've learned in training sessions and apply it on the job to what will most inspire your people to strengthen their skills.

Leave a Lasting Legacy: Be an Effective People Developer
By Robert N. Llewellyn

One might think people development is an obvious characteristic of all successful companies and their managers. But Lominger Limited Inc.— a leadership development think tank and consultancy—reports that managers and employees ranked "developing direct reports" dead last out of all 67 competencies in its biannual study of leadership skills. That's right—managers are viewed and view themselves "worst" at developing their direct reports compared to all other skills in their toolboxes.

Fears and hollow excuses are usually what prevent managers from developing their people. You may not be actively developing your reports' jobs because you fear:

- Losing power. If you develop your people, you may not be the technical expert of your area anymore. (In reality, you agreed to not be the expert any more when you took a leadership position.)

- Losing your good people. As people develop, they may want to grow further beyond the function of your department. Be aware, however, that if you are seen as a "people hoarder," your career will be severely diminished.

- Being "leap-frogged." Someone you develop may eventually get a job you want. You may even have to report to one of your previous direct reports. (Let's hope you developed them well.) If you use this excuse, you're revealing a basic insecurity about your own abilities.

- Creating a rival. Worse than the fear of being leapfrogged may be the fear that a former direct report could become an archrival in your organization. This excuse is another indication of personal insecurity.

Or you may not be developing other leaders because it takes time or because you want to avoid the responsibility. But what else are you doing with your time that is more important? Here are six reasons why you should can the excuses and work on your people-development skills:

- To improve productivity and effectiveness. While developing a direct report may cause some temporary reduction in productivity, it will pay dividends in your department, team or division in the long run.

- To maximize long-term potential. Developing direct reports improves the long-run success of your entire company.

- To keep your sanity. Good people developers usually go home on time. Developing your people not only improves their capacity to perform, but it improves your capacity to delegate.

- To attract talent. When the word gets out that you are a people developer, the up-and-comers in your company line up to work in your department, team, shop or division.

- To "plant" good people. When people leave your area, they know your department's function, your methods and your needs, and can help you be successful from their new positions.

- To get promoted. Being a great people developer differentiates you from the pack. People say good things about you. People realize you are a more complete leader, not the usual one-commodity manager.

No one becomes a great people developer overnight, and there's no one right way to do it. You should cater to your strengths and to your style. Here are some general tips for improvement:

- Be the motivator, not the "mom." Convince your employees that they are responsible for their own development. Each must have a written development plan, including both short- and long-term development goals. Remind employees that capitalism is "creative destruction" and that their jobs may dissolve without notice. Corporate maternalism breeds unhealthy dependence on the company and minimizes self-reliance.

- Incorporate their need to have a personal development plan into your performance-management process.

- Recognize that development is more than going to training. While training courses are an important aspect of development, so are rotations, special tasks, complex projects, reading assignments, informal "brown-bag discussions" and even successful staff meetings.

- Coach with a passion. Most people can remember a coach, teacher or mentor who dared to confront behavior when it was less than optimal. People developers constructively confront—in a private and professional way—when needed.

- Delegate incessantly, and make assignments with development in mind.

- Know your people, particularly their career aspirations.

- When interviewing potential hires for your department, discuss an estimated time for them to move on (assuming this fits their career aspirations), usually by the end of three years. Make moving on a goal, and promise that you will help them find their next position within the company when they have developed to your expectations and performed in their current job for a reasonable period of time.

- Creatively reward people who actively develop themselves. Money is not always the right answer. Know your people and reward them with a motivating intangible.

Training: Make it Stick— and Pay Off
By Kathryn Tyler

You've probably sent way too many staffers off for training with a shrug. What they get out of the training—and what they apply on the job—seems a matter of luck. How would you like to better the odds that they return with meaningful skills that make a difference?

Managers can make a difference, say the experts, in what trainees absorb as well as how they apply what they've learned on the job. For maximum retention, employees need to be eager and ready to learn. The message you convey about the training is crucial in creating the right learning climate.

"Before the training, managers need to sit down and talk with the trainee about why they are enrolled in the class, what they are expected to learn and how they can use it on the job," advises Barbara Carnes, coauthor of *Making Training Stick* (Creative Training Techniques, 1992). Creating that expectation beforehand increases trainees' use of what they learn, she explains.

Second, while you may not control the entire scheduling process of training, you may be able to take some proactive efforts to increase the learning retention factor by observing the following "scheduling" rules:

- The learning curve declines late in the day, and full-day training is less effective than half or three-fourths of a day. The best scheduling is one or two times a week for two or three hours at a time, advises Carnes.

- Avoid training during important monthly meetings where preparation time is heavy. (If you can't change the time of the training, perhaps you can change your monthly meetings during the training cycle.)

- Schedule training as close to the time they need the new skills as possible. If your boss wants everyone trained on a new software program, make sure you have the program installed on staffers' computers before they start the training.

- Decide who should attend the training. Only those who need the training should attend, not those who think they might need it.

- Consider scheduling several employees from one department to take the course at the same time. While this may present difficulties in covering workload, it may be worthwhile in the long run. When trainees have partners who work nearby, they can support each other and solve problems together when they return to the job site, which boosts learning retention.

- Minimize distractions for your staff during training.

"Managers can support the participation of the trainee by helping them with [job] coverage while they're gone, so they are not as stressed," says Carnes. Moreover, "Participants who are interrupted, make phone calls or check voice mail on breaks are not as likely to use what they learned, because their attention is distracted" during the training.

The most crucial point in the training process occurs once employees are back at work. Again, managers have a crucial role.

Ask employees about what they've learned and how they plan to use it in their jobs. "Then check in with them and see if they are using it or if they need any further support," recommends Carnes. Another retention technique: Have attendees teach what they learn to someone else within 24 hours.

One option is to schedule some time for employees to give a short presentation on the training to co-workers during a staff meeting. Bonus: Employees who know they will have to do this exercise probably will pay closer attention to the material and will learn it more thoroughly—and co-workers can share in the participant's new knowledge.

If refresher courses aren't available, try the alternative of "brown-bag dialogues" about the training.

The best way to get people to remember what they've been taught? Get them to use it immediately and consistently upon returning to the workplace by making sure they have the necessary tools and equipment. Then, provide opportunities and a pace of workflow that allows for new skills to be applied.

To Transfer Training to the Workplace, Use It or Lose It
By Jathan W. Janove

Transfer of training begins with a trainer who has ideas, concepts, tools and techniques to teach. Trainees may or may not learn them. But even if they do, "transfer" has not necessarily occurred. The lessons must translate into on-the-job behavior for the training to have transferred. So, what can managers do to improve the workplace through training?

Unlike batteries, toothpicks or snow shovels, training can't be kept in inventory for a long time. It is truly a "use it now or lose it" proposition. Even if you return from a program motivated and excited, you'll still face pre-existing patterns of thought and behavior in the workplace that may work against implementing the new ideas.

For example, if you're motivated to implement a new method for giving employees oral and written feedback, it will change your relationship with your employees. Even though these new methods would benefit everyone, they still involve change. And pre-existing workplace cultural issues may present obstacles to the new management approaches. Even without such obstacles, occasionally you'll have a relapse and default to old behaviors. To avoid this problem and create optimal conditions for transfer to occur, take the following steps:

Become a teacher. By teaching others what you learn from a training program, two things are likely to happen. You'll remember what you learned, and you'll practice what you learned.

Set specific goals or tasks to put into action. For example, if you learned a new approach to giving employees written feedback, establish a goal to document eight feedback sessions in the first month after the training or to write six notes of praise to your employees.

Keep a journal. Record when you have applied the new tools and techniques, the results you obtained, benefits experienced and obstacles encountered.

Use visual or memory aids. A detailed training handout can be useful for review or refreshing memories, but it will probably gather dust. More helpful are charts, cards, models, acronyms and similar devices that quickly, simply and clearly express the core elements of a training concept or technique. Look for and ask for such devices from the trainers and HR professionals. You may develop your own useful aid, such as a card on which you write key words that will prompt you to practice what you were taught.

Get a coach or training partner. This person can be critical to achieving transfer because he can help you recall the lessons taught, reinforce their importance and keep motivation and momentum going. Also, when you encounter obstacles or experience relapses to former behavior patterns, your coach or partner can help you overcome these roadblocks.

Get help from HR. Usually, HR professionals and trainers recognize the importance of the transitional process and already have planned follow-up sessions designed to measure progress, recognize and reward achievement and resolve obstacles. Even if they haven't, you still can ask for help. With a little prodding, you may get needed organizational support, individual coaching or troubleshooting, as well as additional resources such as books and articles to help you develop the selected skills. The key is to ask.

Hands-On Employee Development: A Good Bet to Retain Your Best Workers
By Carla Joinson

If your idea of "employee development" is "classroom training," you're missing the opportunity to excel at your job. Reason: "The greatest employee development comes from managers taking time to develop employees through mentoring, assigning interesting projects and identifying improvement areas," says Michael Simpson, senior consultant in the organization practice at Watson Wyatt Worldwide in San Francisco.

The idea is for managers to serve as coaches and mentors, not taskmasters, says David White, cofounder of Cambridge, Mass.-based Human Capital Technology (a software company making competency-based HR management and development systems) and product manager for that technology with consultant William M. Mercer.

White offers the example of a manager and employee who together decide that the employee needs to gain a competency to be in line for the next promotion. "That employee can volunteer for an on-the-job project, the manager can add more responsibilities to the present job, mentor the employee or offer options like rotation or a lateral move," says White. "It doesn't always have to be 100 percent tuition reimbursement. There are lots of ways to deliver development."

So, with that concept in mind, what's standing in your way? You may think it will take too much time. Another reason: Managers typically don't get negative repercussions for failing to develop employees.

On the other hand, developing your employees should help you keep your best workers. For example, when John Madigan, vice president of HR for The Hartford's 3,500-member IT group in Hartford, Conn., conducted a retention study that surveyed people who left the organization voluntarily, he discovered that 90 percent of those who left voluntarily talked about career and professional development and the level of support their managers gave them in this area. Although the company made courses available to employees, it found that wasn't enough: Workers wanted their managers to help guide them. "What employees wanted," says Madigan, "were managers who were really interested in their development and in mentoring and coaching them. Instead, employees ended up feeling that their managers weren't putting as much effort into developing them as they could."

The Hartford has made it a little easier for managers to develop employees through a Corporate University web site. It "allows both managers and employees to search by competency, subject, course title, vendor and so on," he says. "Managers used to have to spend hours searching through education catalogues and other material to get the same results, which was a disincentive to do it." Madigan says that because employees can access the Corporate University, they end up doing a lot of the background research themselves and come to managers more prepared. "The managers are happier when it happens this way—the process of coaching and providing guidance has become much less onerous."

Madigan also is enthusiastic about a pilot career development platform that was slated to roll out in April 2001. "It's an online system where people can look at 'job families,' see what advancement is out there and then look at what the differences are in expectations, responsibilities and competencies from what they're currently doing," he explains. "This platform allows managers to better articulate why people are at specific levels and what they need to develop to progress within or across job families."

In addition, managers are more willing to get involved with employee development, says Madigan, because the company's study "showed a clear link between managers' active involvement in employee development and the retention of talented individuals. The link was always a bit speculative until we did this."

At The Hartford, IT managers also are appraised on employee development as "a defined part of the 'results expected' that reflects part of their bonus eligibility," Madigan adds. "We believe this communicates how important we think it is."

Madigan says managers can show their success in this area by demonstrating the following:

- The number of people who have gone through development per quarter or year.

- The number of employees who have developmental objectives in their appraisal/review documents.

- The amount of money spent per employee on development and training.

- Positive changes in employee survey responses regarding development and the manager's role in it.

Learn What Motivates Your Employees to Help Them Develop
By Robert N. Llewellyn

The "career concept" is one way to help you better understand your employees and, therefore, get more out of them. This approach is based on the work of Michael Driver, Ph.D., professor of organizational behavior and director of the management assessment program at the Marshall School of Business at the University of Southern California at Los Angeles.

The premise is that everyone has a concept of career success that was programmed into his psyche from as early as childhood or at the beginning of his professional life. Each person's career concept is derived from such things as parents and family, national culture, company culture, a mentor or even birth order.

The framework posits that there are four distinct career concepts. Each is unique, and no single career concept is right for everyone. Of the four, the first two have been intuitively known for some time; the final two more recently have been recognized and apply to many people in the workplace.

- **Linear.** To the person motivated by the linear concept, success only comes from moving up the corporate ladder. While prevalent in the United States, this proves to be a difficult concept to yield continuing success. Movement up the organizational pyramid provides fewer positions into which to advance. Many who carry the linear concept are frustrated. Many leave positions of influence when they become "topped out." The "de-layering" of organizational levels of the 1990s left many linears disillusioned. For many, it is an emotionally brutal concept.

- **Expert.** Success for the person motivated by the expert concept is being known as the best among his or her peers. This includes the craft worker who yearns to be the best welder at Amalgamated Inc. It is also the trial lawyer garnering community recognition for a high-profile case, the surgeon with national recognition for an innovative procedure or the accountant with the most knowledge in the department of accounting rules. Those who carry the expert concept may have been told in their youth to "grow up to be good at something." Their parents or grandparents may have been influenced by the Great Depression, during which the employees who kept their jobs were often the ones with the best skills.

- **Spiral.** Success is being able to move from one position to a related but often broader position, usually every five to 10 years. Broadening is the key. A spiral's parents may have taught him to be "well rounded." New positions are a natural extension of the prior work. This is the engineer who migrates into project management and then to capital budgeting and eventually to corporate budgeting functions. Spirals amass a vast amount of knowledge and experience. Many spirals in mid-career feel a strong desire to share the massive knowledge with others. This leads some spirals to leave large companies to become consultants or teachers.

- **Roamer.** Success to the roamer is being able to change jobs often. Movement is more frequent than spirals, perhaps every two to three years, and the succeeding jobs are often unrelated to past professional experiences. A roamer may move from funeral director to draftsman. These are often people from the extremes of economic backgrounds who don't value security. They either were raised in an upper-economic stratum and presume money will always be there or were in a poorer economic environment and know they can survive on very little. Roamers can play key roles in companies that are expanding, both geographically and into new markets. They make good startup people. Roamers tend to value work with high people involvement.

Each career concept has a set of underlying motives—the things that make people happy at work and energize them. Linears are motivated by power and achievement. Experts seek expertise and security. Spirals value growth and creativity. Roamers are passionate about variety and independence.

Unfortunately, many people have a particular concept of career success wired into their belief system, but they have strong underlying motives that tie to another concept. Such a misalignment between concept and motives could lead to chronic dysfunctions, such as discord, despair, lack of motivation, cynicism and frustration. If an employee has a set of motives that do not fit his concept of career success, he can more easily change his concept of success than the underlying motives to achieve alignment and end these dysfunctional feelings and behaviors.

How do you apply this framework to your everyday management? First, find out your employees' career concepts and motives, and then take action. During formal performance assessments, managers should include the need for each direct report to provide a personal development plan for both short-term and long-term planning horizons. Look here for clues of each person's career concept.

One-on-one informal discussions are also usually more valuable than formal reviews. The former provide open dialogue outside of the formal performance management time between you and your direct reports on development and particularly career perceptions. Good people developers schedule such meetings regularly. Managers easily can ask a revealing question: "How do you become successful at this company?" An employee's response should divulge much about his career concept, not necessarily his underlying motives. More probing open-ended questions may be necessary to understand the employee's motives: "What type of work makes you feel proud?" "What has brought you the most satisfaction at work recently?" or "What gets your motor revved up each morning?"

Once you determine which career concept fits each employee, you can begin to develop each one accordingly. For instance, for those with linear motives, managers can provide leadership training; delegate leadership skills-building opportunities, such as budget preparation; and provide projects in which an employee can test and hone his leadership skills.

For employees with expert motives, managers should provide training that deepens their expertise. Experts can be encouraged to write for industry journals and attend related technical conferences. Experts should be warned that the market may eventually not value their expertise and flexibility in such events. They may even have to find new areas of expertise to develop.

With an employee who has spiral motives, managers should look for rotations requiring broader skills. Special creative projects in new areas of the company, particularly those on cross-functional teams, also are good assignments.

And finally, for those with roamer motives, managers should plan for these employees to move on at agreed-upon times after they have had a chance to contribute to the department. Managers should be aware of company strategic moves and communicate them to roamers who like to be involved in something new.

For the linears, spirals and roamers, managers should strike a deal to "advertise" for these employees after they have had sufficient experience and performance in their current job. Yes, people developers lose good people. They also have a long line of good people clamoring to transfer in.

Four Career Paths

Path Type	Employee defines success as . . .	Example	To develop this employee . . .
Linear	Moving up the corporate ladder.	George starts off as a sales representative and eventually becomes regional sales manager, division manager and then general manager.	• Provide leadership training. • Delegate leadership skill-building opportunities (e.g., budget preparation). • Provide projects that test leadership skills.
Expert	Being known as the best among his or her peers.	Sarah, an accountant, becomes the person in the company who knows the most about accounting rules.	• Provide training that deepens his or her expertise. • Encourage employee to write for industry journals and attend trade conferences.
Spiral	Broadening his or her skills through job changes every 5 to 10 years.	Hakkan, an engineer, migrates into project management and then capital budgeting and eventually into corporate budgeting.	• Look for rotations requiring broadened skills. • Encourage employee to participate in cross-functional teams handling special creative projects in new areas of the company.
Roamer	Exploring a variety of unrelated jobs often, perhaps every 2 to 3 years.	Mina works for several years as a graphic designer, then gets a job in the development office of a not-for-profit and next goes into freelance marketing writing.	• Plan for employee to move on after an agreed-upon time after he or she has contributed to your department. • Communicate the company's strategic moves.

Quick Tips for Strengthening Your People's Skills

- Think that sending your people to training is the best way to develop their skills? Professional development opportunities take many different forms in addition to formal training. These include rotations, special tasks, complex projects, reading assignments and informal "brown-bag" discussions.

- Wondering how to help employees retain what they've learned during a training session? Immediately after the session, ask them what they've learned and how they plan to use it in their jobs. Check in to see if they need support in applying their new learning. And invite them to give a short presentation to co-workers on what they've learned.

- Need additional suggestions to help employees apply new learning on the job? Encourage your people to establish a goal to use their new knowledge in the workplace in specific ways by a certain date. Advise them to record how they've used new tools and techniques, what worked well and what didn't and what changes they might make to get more from their training in the future.

- Want to customize your professional-development efforts to each employee? Identify their ideal career path, then provide them with the right opportunities. For example, does Harry view success as climbing the corporate ladder? If so, provide him with leadership training and assignments (such as budget preparation) that hone his leadership skills.

- Need additional ideas for developing employees' on-the-job skills? Consider suggesting a company web site that enables people to look at "job families," see what advancement is out there, and look at the differences in expectations, responsibilities and competencies from what they're currently doing.

SECTION FIVE:
ASSESSING WORKERS' PERFORMANCE

As a manager, you can't discern how well your employees' on-the-job activities are supporting your organization's mission unless you establish a rigorous process for evaluating their performance. Yet conducting performance appraisals counts among many managers' most dreaded tasks.

Help is at hand. In the articles that follow, you'll find strategies for augmenting formal performance appraisals with frequent, informal exchanges that keep employees on track, addressing the often inherently subjective nature of performance evaluations, and tackling additional challenges associated with assessing workers' on-the-job results.

Make Performance Appraisals Part of Your Weekly Routine
By Deborah Keary

Giving performance appraisals is a universally hated task but one of the most important tasks you will undertake as a manager. That's why it is so important that you don't allow the time crunch in the workplace—or any other reason—to get in the way of giving timely feedback to your staff. Otherwise, you run the risk of giving out-of-date feedback or feedback that often ends up being a big, unwelcome surprise to your employee.

Annual performance feedback just won't do the trick; the performance appraisal process should be happening all year long. But the good news is that it doesn't have to be a formal process. Weekly or monthly chats with each employee on how things are going can go a long way to building performance appraisal into your routine. These regular informal exchanges also give you the opportunity to review any recent critical incidents. You can discuss those things that went badly and those things that went well, and the role the employee played in both productive and nonproductive incidents while the time period is still fresh in everyone's mind.

Here's another reason for these timely interchanges: They can help you identify the need for training or career development for your employees and give them opportunities to improve poor performance. They also can give you an opportunity to take note of excellent performance that may lead to bonuses, awards or merit increases, as well as the opportunity to document poor performance that may lead ultimately to disciplinary action.

In addition, these brief and informal discussions are a great time for you to get feedback from your staff. Many employees have good ideas about processes and products and how things could be improved at work if they are given an opportunity to contribute. An atmosphere of open two-way communications will help your employees feel comfortable with offering suggestions or bringing problems to your attention.

What deters many managers from having such discussions with employees is that poor performance occurs because most people neither give nor respond well to criticism. But if you present routine objective performance facts openly and positively—and avoid attacking employees on a personal level—they'll be more likely to respond more positively when you present them with the facts and ask for suggestions to improve the situation.

If you take this one step further and keep a simple log of conversations held with your employees each week or month, over the year you'll develop a performance record for each of your employees, with examples of individual progress or lack thereof. When that dreaded annual performance review day arrives, you'll have documentation readily available that already has been discussed with employees. The record will show improvement or the lack of improvement, training opportunities pursued and whether goals were met or missed. There won't be any surprises for either party, and the performance discussion can be smooth and productive—and a lot less work for you.

Fine-Tune Performance Appraisals to Make Them Effective—and Less Arduous
By Jonathan A. Segal

You may not like performance appraisals—few people do. But they provide so many important benefits, legal and otherwise, for both managers and employers, that despite their recent bad press, they need to be enhanced, rather than ignored. For a start, think about these benefits provided by appraisal systems:

Communicating deficiencies. If under-performing workers are terminated without being given a chance to improve, they will perceive the discharge to be unfair. While unfairness is not unlawful, it can motivate employees to take legal action. And even the most pedestrian plaintiff's lawyer can turn an unfair treatment claim into a viable discrimination or wrongful discharge claim by arguing that the employee was fired for belonging to a protected group (such as age) or for engaging in a protected activity (such as complaining about harassment).

Ensuring consistency. Discrimination complaints often allege that employees with similar performance levels were handed dissimilar rewards or discipline. A good performance appraisal instrument increases the potential for consistency by ensuring that all similarly situated employees are evaluated on the same criteria.

Distinguishing among employees. Performance appraisals that are consistently applied throughout the organization can help employers pinpoint the strongest—and weakest—employees. They also can help justify in court, if necessary, any positive or negative personnel actions taken.

Recognizing valued performers. Even in the best companies, attitude surveys often reveal employee complaints about lack of appreciation and recognition. The performance appraisal lets top performers know concretely of their value to the organization and improves retention.

Communicating strategic vision. Employee goals need to be tied to the organization's broad strategic aims. For example, an organization that values diversity can reflect this by evaluating supervisory personnel on their sensitivity to and appreciation of diversity. When properly executed, an appraisal instrument can become a powerful tool for establishing corporate culture and ensuring that employees understand and act on the organization's broad strategic goals.

Given all these benefits, what seems to be the problem? Most complaints about performance appraisals center on the following:

• They discourage teamwork/collaboration.

• They're inconsistent.

• They're valuable only at the extremes.

• They're too short-term oriented.

• They're autocratic.

• They're too subjective.

• They produce emotional anguish.

These complaints can be valid, but they also can be remedied. For example, if collaboration is essential, make it a criterion on which employees are evaluated. Appraisals that focus on—and reward—collaborative behavior will encourage teamwork. Conversely, appraisals that punish employees for working contrary to the team, such as withholding information, discourage anti-collaborative behaviors.

Here are some solutions to other "problems" with performance appraisals.

Problem: Inconsistency

Solution: When managers are planning a negative ranking, they should ask themselves: "Does any other employee whom I supervise have the same or a similar deficiency?" If so, the employee in the current situation should receive the same or a similar ranking. It also helps to evaluate all employees at the same time each year (as opposed to throughout the year on employees' anniversary dates). This makes it more likely that you will apply the same criteria or factors.

Problem: Valuable only at the extremes

Solution: Include a question that compares performance, such as "Is the employee's overall performance generally stronger than, the same as or weaker than others performing the same or similar tasks?" This question can be particularly useful when you are asked to rank all subordinates on whether they are "meeting expectations" because you can assign a loose ranking to .employees who are performing satisfactorily but to different degrees.

Problem: Short-term orientation

Solution: Include both short-term and long-term goals for decision-makers. Those who excel at one but not the other are not meeting expectations. To minimize legal risk, when discussing long-range plans, always focus on the company, the department or the product line—not the employee. For example, it is legally safer to say, "How should this process work in three years?" rather than "How will you be running this process in three years?" Also, the appraisal process should be dovetailed with the compensation program to encourage employees to seek more than short-term goals.

Problem: Autocratic

Solution: Make sure the appraisal is not one-sided by asking employees for their comments on their appraisals. This also helps managers understand how employees perceive themselves. Don't limit employee comments to written form. If the process is interactive, employees are more likely to understand their evaluations and you are more likely to understand their perception of their limitations.

Problem: Too subjective

Solution: Measure achievement in terms of specific behaviors, rather than general personality traits, to increase objectivity. For example, if adaptability is essential to the job, look for specific behaviors that either confirm or contradict the employee's ability to deal with ambiguity, shift gears quickly, see the big picture quickly, make decisions without "perfect" information and value diverse ways of handling problems.

Problem: Emotional anguish

Solution: First, minimize emotional anguish by conducting reviews on time. The longer employees wait for a review, the more anxious they become. And deliver criticism in a constructive, nonpunitive way. And to the extent that appraisals create anguish in those who don't meet expectations, that's not a bad thing. It may stimulate them to leave on their own initiative. And employees who leave on their own are less likely to sue.

Not-So-Difficult Solutions for Not-So-Easy Performance Appraisals
By Dick Grote

Even the best managers sometimes face difficult challenges in giving performance appraisals. What do you do when a subordinate doesn't work in your location? How do you handle a subordinate who has more technical knowledge? Or, in what is perhaps the most difficult situation, how do you cope with a poorly performing subordinate who thinks she's a star?

Typical training programs skirt those troublesome questions, but you can overcome these and other tough situations if you learn to concentrate on—and deliver—the single, most important message you want to communicate. Here are some examples:

You're at headquarters in Cincinnati; Mary runs the regional office in Des Moines. You only meet face to face during her quarterly corporate visits and your occasional travels to Iowa. While you still have to appraise her performance, you don't have to figure out how. Make it her job—by giving it to her.

Before the appraisal cycle, explain the dilemma: "Mary, one of the challenges we face is that I'm responsible for doing your performance appraisal and yet we don't have much contact with each other. I need you to come up with a plan that will allow me to get all of the information I need to do an honest job of evaluating your performance. Over the next couple of weeks I would like you to figure out how I will be able to get a complete picture of the contributions you are making." The quality of Mary's plan then becomes another factor to consider in assessing her performance.

Here's Janet's problem: She was named director of an important project because of her excellent marketing and management skills, but half the people she supervises are technical whizzes who know far more about the operation of the system.

She could start with a similar approach to that used when you're geographically remote: "Bob, I'm the manager of this department, but you are far more technically adept than I will ever be. In addition to doing world class technical work, I need for you to educate me in how to recognize world class work when I see it. I want you to come up with a plan."

A group-effort assignment could be another approach to this problem. Gather all the team members and explain that one of their assignments is "boss education." You're holding them accountable for teaching you how to accurately evaluate the quality of their work. Don't be surprised if a peer review process is recommended. That's probably the best—and the fairest—solution they could devise.

While most poor performers know that they're missing the mark, a few are adamantly out of touch with reality. Take Sally: She thinks she's a star; you, and everyone else, know she's falling short.

In this situation, it's smart to disregard much of the normal advice about giving performance appraisals. For example, while it's normally wise to ask people to write a self appraisal, it's not in this case. You don't want to encourage Sally to make her inflated opinion of her performance even more intractable by writing her version down on an appraisal form—unless company policy requires everyone to create a self appraisal.

So, how should you break the bad news? Here, being blunt is a virtue. Say, "Come in, Sally, and sit down. I have some bad news for you. I have your performance appraisal here and, quite frankly, it isn't very good. I'd like you to read it, and then let's talk about where we go from here."

Don't get your hopes up that Sally will read all the unpleasantly accurate things you have written about her and immediately vow to change her ways. She may ultimately do that, but there will be some struggle along the way.

Typically, employees fight or take flight. The fight response is the easiest to spot. Someone might raise his voice, pound the desk, point his finger or fold his arms across his chest and stare.

The "flight" defensive reaction is more difficult to pick up. The person will look or turn away, become quieter and speak more slowly than usual. The person also might change the subject or ask for less information than you might reasonably expect.

A telltale sign of a flight reaction is premature agreement. Too often, though, managers accept hasty agreements and fail to ensure that the message has been fully received. The abrupt agreement isn't genuine or sincere; it's a mechanism used to bring this distressing situation to an end and get away.

The best strategy for dealing with defensiveness is first to recognize that it's a normal human reaction. Second, allow the person to vent and listen carefully. Then, agree with anything said that is factually accurate. People can't argue with people who agree with them.

Next, restate the person's position. Say something like, "If I understand what you're saying, Sally, you feel that . . ." Many times, just having someone accurately hear what they say is sufficient to make their defensiveness vanish.

It's also important to deal with an excuse. While it may not be a conscious choice, any time a person offers an excuse for poor performance, he is trying to absolve himself of personal responsibility. Our response needs to focus not on the excuse but on the issue of personal responsibility.

Agree with the fact of the excuse: "I agree, Mark. Having deadlines that frequently change in the middle of a project does make your work difficult." Then, put the responsibility back where it belongs: "And as we have discussed before, changing deadlines is a fact of life in our business. How are you planning to handle that challenge so that you can make sure that your projects are always ready when they're needed?"

While discussion difficulties can be dealt with and solved on an individual basis, the most powerful tool you can have to handle any appraisal challenge is a clear core message. That's the most important point you want to communicate to the employee. If you are clear on that, discussion difficulties will take care of themselves.

Tips for Handling
Tricky Performance Appraisals

Are you reviewing...	Try this strategy...
An employee who doesn't work in your location?	Ask the person for suggestions on how you can get all the information you need to evaluate his or her on-the-job contributions.
A subordinate who has more technical knowledge than you do?	Invite the employee to educate you on how to evaluate technical skills. A peer-review process might help.
A poorly performing direct report who's certain he or she is a star?	Deliver the bad news in no uncertain terms, ask the person to read the performance review, and initiate discussion about where to go from there.

A Step-by-Step Guide to Performance Documents
By Brent Roper

When it comes to reprimands and terminations, treat each employee as if he might file a lawsuit. Reason: He might. And while you cannot control the legal system or juries, you can control the facts.

Believe it or not, most cases turn on the facts. It is crucial to have facts that are in your favor and to establish the circumstances of the case in writing. In any employment lawsuit that arises out of a termination for poor performance, one of the most important factual elements is what is said between the manager and the employee. Unfortunately, in nearly every lawsuit of this type, there is a huge difference between the accounts of the two parties on what was actually verbally said.

That's why written documentation regarding employee performance is so crucial to defend yourself and your organization. When written documentation is done well, defense attorneys find it difficult to dispute.

At the same time, the purpose of all informal feedback, performance coaching and formal documentation of employee performance issues should be to rehabilitate the employee's behavior and to work with the employee to correct and raise his or her level of performance to an acceptable level. The purpose of feedback, coaching and formal documentation is never to punish the employee or to prepare documents for the sole purpose of terminating the employee.

A well-written appraisal of performance is the best way to get the employee's attention and warn him that a problem exists and he needs to correct it. The following guidelines should help you do just that.

- Address the memo to the employee. Include the current date and note the subject of the memo as "job performance." Employees should see the documents as coming from the manager.

- Be courteous and professional. It's fine to say that the employee's behavior is unacceptable or below standard, but managers should not use demeaning or hostile words. Stick to the facts and exclude your feelings about the matter. Again, you do not want to include anything that could inflame a jury.

- Include a short introduction. The introduction should state the purpose of the memo—that there are problems with the employee's performance and that corrective action is necessary.

- Bullet each specific area of a performance problem. Instead of randomly covering various areas of the employee's performance in the document, prepare a bullet point for each area where the employee's performance needs to improve. Then, elaborate as necessary under each bullet point regarding the specifics. By scanning the bullet points in the document the employee (or juror) can quickly tell what areas need to be corrected. Doing this also makes the document easier to read and easier to later find information in the document. For each bullet point, state the following:

1. The behavior that needs to be corrected, specific examples of the behavior and any policy that was violated. Include as many facts as possible, be precise and, when possible, include dates, times, names, specific facts, other people involved, etc. Also, if an employee has violated an organization's policy (such as a policy written out in an employee handbook), state the policy and how it was violated.

2. A brief history of past coaching or counseling—or how you got to this point. Include whether you have repeatedly spoken to the employee about a matter, wrote it up in a performance appraisal and otherwise coached the employee on the issue. That helps the employee, as well as a potential

juror, understand that the problem has been occurring for a period of time and that you have been working with the employee to correct the issue.

3. Include the employee's side of the story and then evaluate the behavior. It is helpful to have spoken to the employee about the matter before actually writing the formal document regarding an employee's performance. This allows you to understand and consider the employee's side. Then, in the formal write-up, briefly include the employee's view and a couple of sentences as to why or why not the employee acted appropriately. Many employees get upset because managers do not consider all of the facts of a situation or never ask them for their side. This technique forces you to talk to the employee, to consider the employee's side and then "evaluate" or decide if the employee's side has merit. Again, it helps the employee understand what he or she did wrong. This is also important when the document is given to a jury or fact-finder to consider. On the face of the document, it appears that the manager acted fairly and appropriately and reasonably and was interested in the employee's side of the matter and considered it.

4. Include the impact of the employee's poor performance. For example, if you write, "Your lack of follow-up regarding a customer request led to the customer not making a $20,000 order," it demonstrates how the organization was affected by an employee's poor performance. It also shows employees "why" they need to have good performance and sets forth the organization's business reason for taking action. It also shows the fact-finder that the performance was below standard. If this aspect is left out of the document, the fact-finder does not fully understand the importance of the poor performance.

5. State exactly what behavior the employee must do to correct the problem. For example, by writing, "In the future you should not yell at customers and you must treat all customers professionally, courteously and respectfully," you set out exactly what the employee must do and show what good behavior "looks like." Also, in thinking about corrective action, consider whether the employee can benefit from additional training,

either internal or external. Training is another sign that fact-finders look to regarding whether a manager was really trying to help an employee or was actually trying to terminate them due to an ill motive. If you can give the employee additional training, do it; it demonstrates to the fact-finder that you went above and beyond to try and help the employee.

6. State what will happen to the employee if the performance issues are not corrected. For example, if you write, "Failure to correct this will result in further disciplinary action up to and including termination," the employee can't fail to get the message. Sometimes, managers do not wish to include this language because it makes the document sound "hard." The bottom line: Employees need to understand the importance of the issue. It is not fair to the employee to terminate them for something without appropriate warnings (unless the conduct is extreme, such as stealing or some other clear and serious policy violation). This is also something that can inflame juries. To summarily terminate an employee without notice and without cause may swing sympathies toward the employee.

7. State when follow-up/feedback will occur. It is not fair to the employee to hang the performance issue over his or her head for an indefinite period of time. It is also important to periodically tell the employee where he or she is regarding their performance and to give him or her reasonable feedback. For example, you could say, "We will review your performance in 30, 60 and 90 days or as soon as necessary." If you include the date of the follow-up, it is extremely important to perform and document the follow-up.

8. End the memo on a positive note and agree to answer questions or otherwise assist the employee. You want to leave the reader with the impression that this is not personal and that the employee was treated professionally and with respect.

9. Require the employee to sign the document. This establishes that he or she received it and cannot later claim that he or she did not receive it. If an employee refuses to sign, then just write "Employee received this document but refused to sign."

Your Performance-Document Checklist

You're considering reprimanding or terminating an employee for poor performance. And you've prepared a written memo detailing the problem and the attempts made so far to correct it. Check whether the memo satisfies the crucial criteria listed below.

The performance memo ...	Yes	No
1. Is addressed to the employee in question.	❑	❑
2. Has a courteous and professional tone.	❑	❑
3. Sticks to the facts and excludes emotions.	❑	❑
4. Starts with a short introduction stating the purpose of the memo: to identify performance problems and the need for corrective action.	❑	❑
5. Contains a bullet point for each performance area where the employee needs to improve.	❑	❑
6. Identifies behaviors that need correcting and provides specific examples.	❑	❑
7. Includes a brief history of coaching, counseling, previous remedial conversations and other attempts to address problem performance.	❑	❑
8. Contains a brief description of the employee's view of the situation.	❑	❑
9. Provides a description of the impact of the employee's poor performance on the company.	❑	❑
10. States what exactly the employee must do to correct the problem and by when.	❑	❑
11. States what will happen to the employee if performance problems aren't corrected on schedule.	❑	❑
12. Stipulates when a follow-up conversation or feedback will take place.	❑	❑
13. Ends on a positive note and an offer to answer questions.	❑	❑

Sample Employee Performance Document

Comments
document
To the employee
From manager

MEMORANDUM

To: John Doe, [Job Title]

From: Sally Smith, [Manager / Job Title]

Date: Current Date

The document should be close in time (not more than a few weeks) from when the poor performance occurred.

Subject: Job Performance

Message:
Recently, several areas regarding your job performance have come to my attention. It is absolutely necessary that your performance in the areas outlined herein immediately improve. This memo sets forth the specific problems, what effect they are having on the organization and what you can do to correct the problems.

Introduction – explain what the purpose of the memo is.

Bullet each item where performance needs to improve.

Brief history of the problem, including when the manager previously has addressed the issue.

• **Poor Communication/Poor Customer Service**
In your last performance appraisal of Jan. 1, 200X, the appraisal noted several problems regarding your lack of effective communication. The appraisal specifically mentioned customers complaining of how you treated them and problems getting along with several team members. You were rated a "Fair" under the Communication category. Since that time, I have spoken with you numerous times regarding communication problems, specifically on Nov. 15, Nov. 29 and Dec. 14. Unfortunately I have not seen significant improvement in this area and problems continue to arise.

State EXACTLY what the behavior is, including all relevant facts (names, dates, times, behaviors, words, actions, etc.). Include policies that were violated if any.

On Dec. 27, you took a call from Judy Edwards, assistant vice president for UID, Inc. Ms. Edwards requested that you send her information regarding the investment product you are working on. Ms. Edwards indicated that you told her that you were busy, that you did not have time to talk to her, that she would not understand the product anyway, that she should contact someone else and then you hung up. Ms. Edwards indicated that she then left you three voice mails and two e-mails, to which you never replied.

	After I received an irate call from Ms. Edwards on Dec. 29, I spoke to you about it that same day. You indicated that you had spoken with her on Dec. 27, that you did tell her you were busy, that you may have cursed at her once and that she probably should talk to someone in her department. You indicated that you did not remember telling her that she would not understand the issue. You did remember hanging up on her and not returning her voice mails and e-mails.

Include the employee's side of events.

After I received an irate call from Ms. Edwards on Dec. 29, I spoke to you about it that same day. You indicated that you had spoken with her on Dec. 27, that you did tell her you were busy, that you may have cursed at her once and that she probably should talk to someone in her department. You indicated that you did not remember telling her that she would not understand the issue. You did remember hanging up on her and not returning her voice mails and e-mails.

Include organization policies that were violated.

The company's Employee Behavior policy (see the Employee Handbook at page 28) states: "It is the company's policy that certain rules and regulations regarding employee behavior are necessary for the efficient operation of the company and for the benefit and protection of the rights and safety of all employees. Conduct that interferes with operations or brings discredit to the company will not be tolerated.

"Evaluate" the behavior after considering the employee's side.

Even assuming your version is correct, your actions were unacceptable and violated the company's Employee Behavior policy. All employees must support our customers. It is extremely important that we give professional, courteous support to every customer. You admitted telling Ms. Edwards that you were too busy, cursed at her, hung up on her and did not return her calls or e-mails. These are all examples of poor communication, poor customer service and such conduct clearly brought discredit to the company.

State what the impact or consequences of the employee's behavior is.

The impact of your behavior is that Ms. Edwards has now pulled UID, Inc.'s business, worth approximately $25,000 a year with our company, and is apparently moving their business to our chief competitor. Since UID is a long-time customer of ours—having done more than $200,000 worth of business with us over the last 10 years—this is extremely costly to the company. As you know, our marketing efforts seek to differentiate us from our competitors based on our outstanding customer service. If we are to survive in this competitive market we must deliver outstanding service to our customers. We can ill afford to lose good customers like Ms. Edwards due to your poor customer service.

State what corrective action is necessary to bring the performance issue up to an acceptable level.

Corrective Action on this will be for you to treat all customers (internal or external), particularly those from state insurance departments, professionally, courteously and patiently. It is expected that you will return all customer voice mails and e-mails within 24 hours. If you cannot do this, you must contact me and let me know why. You must also refrain from cursing at customers and talking down to them in a demeaning manner. In the next 60 days you must attend either an internal or external seminar/training on communication/ customer service. I also expect you to contact Ms. Edwards and apologize for your poor behavior.

Consequences if performance issue continues.

If your behavior regarding communication/customer service with internal and external customers does not drastically and immediately improve, you will be subject to further disciplinary action up to and including termination.

If there were more bullet items regarding additional performance issues they would be included here.

Follow-up/feedback

I will review your performance in approximately 30, 60 and 90 days or sooner, as needed. I will be sending you meeting notices for Feb. 1, March 1 and April 1.

Allow employee to ask questions and end courteously.

Please let me know if you have any questions. As you know, I have always tried to work with you in the past and look forward to working with you to resolve these issues. Thank you.

Employee Signature (Indicating Receipt Only):
_____ Date: _____

Watch What You Write When Documenting Employee Performance
By Paul Falcone

Employment pundits and labor attorneys commonly advise managers to "document, document, document." The only part of the message that often gets short shrift is the key fact that if something is worth documenting, it's probably worth sharing with the employee at that particular time. Otherwise, as a manager, you will end up creating a diary of substandard performance issues that serves neither as a training tool nor as documentation that could later be used to justify a dismissal and protect your company from a wrongful termination charge.

If communicating and sharing documentation regarding performance with employees is an essential responsibility of management, then you have to be sure that what you're writing—whether positive or negative—won't come back to haunt you. In addition, documenting performance also has some uncommon pitfalls that you need to take care to avoid.

First, remember that written documents that are not properly designated as "attorney-client privileged" may be subpoenaed by plaintiff attorneys looking for evidence against your company. From that standpoint, performance documentation can be seen as a long-term liability to the corporation. E-mails in particular present a treasure trove of opportunities to litigators because electronic records can never really be destroyed. It's probably easiest to think of the "e" in e-mail as "evidence."

Marking a document "attorney-client privileged" isn't enough to protect it from discovery. Although there are a number of legal issues that make a document privileged, there are a few basic rules that will help you toward that goal. "For a document to be privileged, you need the active involvement of an attorney who is asked to provide an opinion and/or analyze the employer's intended course of action," says Ann Kotlarski, employment litigation partner at Seyfarth Shaw LLC in Los Angeles. "In essence, you have to separate the factual investigation from the legal analysis. When attorneys are asked to provide a legal analysis, there's a greater chance that a court will determine that the document is privileged, which simply means that the document is not admissible as evidence in a courtroom."

Furthermore, the document should have a limited audience, and only those non-attorneys with an absolute need to know should be included in the distribution list. Otherwise, a court might rule that the document is common enough to be shared with a jury.

A key way to ensure that you're protecting a confidential hard-copy document or e-mail is to write "Privileged and confidential: Attorney-client protected communication" at the top of the written page or in the subject line of the e-mail. Address the memo to either your in-house attorney or to your outside counsel. At the end of the document, Kotlarski says, add, "Please give me your legal analysis in terms of the appropriate course of action that we should consider at this point."

Remember, though, that what's considered confidential or privileged is subject to debate, and ultimately a judge will decide what will be admissible as evidence in court. When in doubt, check with qualified employment counsel. It goes without saying that such documentation must be kept outside of a worker's personnel file.

Performance reviews represent another lurking danger for unsuspecting managers. The path of least resistance is avoidance, and rather than addressing performance problems honestly and directly, many managers avoid confrontation by overinflating grades. In an attempt to justify their actions, they often give substandard performers lower scores than the rest of the staff, even if the overall score is still a passing grade. For example, with a grading system showing 5 is superior, 3 meets expectations, and 1 fails to meet expectations, supervisors may give 3s to substandard performers when all other staff members receive 5s.

Those supervisors rationalize, "Well, the individual received a lower score than everyone else on the staff, so he must realize that he's not performing up to par." Similarly, unsuspecting managers give substandard scores in particular performance areas on the review, while still giving an overall acceptable score at the end of the appraisal.

There are two problems here. First, performance reviews are not relative; they're absolute. If the company deems a 3 an acceptable score, then the employee hears that she's met expectations. In a court, that individual may state that she realized that she scored lower than everyone else in the department or that she had no idea what scores the others received. In either case, her lawyer's argument will simply state that she didn't realize that her job was in jeopardy because her overall score for that entire year was acceptable.

Likewise, most performance appraisal forms have nine or 10 individual categories in addition to the overall score at the end. Substandard scores in individual categories will certainly help your case if you're forced to defend a termination, but in and of themselves, they are not an absolute defense. Instead, a failing overall score at the end of the appraisal form must be documented to reflect unacceptable performance for the entire review period.

Here's a simple litmus test to follow when doling out overall scores in the performance review process: If you have any remote hesitations about an individual's ability to make it in your department or company in the upcoming year because of subpar job performance, then you should grade the individual as "not meeting expectations" in the overall score section at the end of the performance appraisal form. Otherwise, the positive record you create today will make it harder to terminate the individual tomorrow.

Progressive disciplinary warnings are especially subject to severe legal scrutiny. There are three key errors that supervisors make when documenting substandard performance or inappropriate workplace conduct in the form of written warnings:

1. Documenting vague and ambiguous consequences at the end of the memo.

For example, generic consequences that refer to subjecting a worker to "further action" or "serious discipline" may very likely leave an employee feeling unsure of your intentions. Worse, if you terminate someone relying on "consequence" language that is particularly vague, a judge or arbitrator may rule that the employee didn't realize that his job was in serious jeopardy of being lost. Instead, conclude disciplinary warnings with the language, "Failure to provide immediate and sustained improvement may result in further disciplinary action up to and including dismissal." This provides you with ample discretion while clearly confirming the seriousness of the consequences to come should the individual's performance not improve to some predetermined standard.

2. "Codifying the damage" when documenting discipline.

Many a well-meaning supervisor has unintentionally placed the organization at risk in an attempt to teach an errant employee a lesson. For example, documenting that an employee has "sexually harassed" a co-worker or "compromised an entire pool of mortgage loans" could later be used against your company as a documented fact. As a term of the trade, "sexual harassment" is a legal conclusion; if you confirm in writing that sexual harassment indeed has occurred, then your own documentation may become prime fodder for a plaintiff attorney looking to find proof of a supervisor's inappropriate actions. Instead, adapt a practice of documenting such matters using language that is less concrete. For example, in the case of a harassment issue where it appears that a supervisor has violated company policy, write: "Your actions appear to violate company policy 5.30." You might also write: "Your actions suggest that you may have created an offensive environment, and I expect you to never again engage in conduct that could appear to diminish a person's self-worth or sense of well-being."

3. Documenting state-of-mind offenses.

In particularly egregious cases of inappropriate workplace conduct, managers sometimes attempt to paint a picture of the severity of the offense by using terms such as "deliberately, purposely, intentionally, willfully and maliciously." Such mental element qualifiers may indeed strengthen your written message to the worker, but they may also unintentionally escalate the written warning so that it appears as a personal attack and may trigger a whole new set of legal challenges.

Quick Tips for Assessing Workers' Performance

- Do you dread conducting annual performance reviews? Conduct regular (weekly or monthly) informal exchanges with employees about their performance. Identify areas for improvement and note excellent performance. Invite ideas from employees about how to improve things at work. And keep a simple log of these exchanges. When annual performance review time rolls around, neither of you will be subjected to any surprises.

- Think performance appraisals are fatally flawed? Tackle those flaws head-on. For example, to correct subjectivity in your appraisal of an employee, measure achievement in terms of specific behaviors, not general personality traits. And to avoid inflicting emotional anguish on employees, conduct appraisals on time.

- Facing special challenges in a particular performance appraisal? For instance, are you reviewing a subordinate who works offsite? An employee who has more technical knowledge than you? A direct report who's performing poorly—but thinks he's a star? Concentrate on—and deliver—the single most important message you want to communicate. For example, "Bob, you're far more technical than I'll ever be. I need you to educate me on how to recognize world-class technical work when I see it."

- Are you considering reprimanding an employee for poor performance or terminating the employment relationship? Compile detailed written documentation of the problem performance and steps taken to try to correct it, and send performance memos to the employee in question. If the person files a lawsuit, you'll have the facts handy to defend your decision.

- Wondering how to document problem behavior in ways that protect your company if the employee sues for wrongful dismissal? Instead of concluding disciplinary warnings with vague language about "further action," use specific language: "Failure to provide immediate and sustained improvement may result in further disciplinary action up to and including dismissal." Instead of stating that an employee "sexually harassed" someone, write: "Your actions appear to violate company policy 5.30." And avoid language such as "You maliciously engaged in destructive conduct;" it appears as a personal attack.

SECTION SIX:
ADDRESSING PROBLEM
BEHAVIOR IN YOUR TEAM

It's one of those unpleasant facts of business life: No matter how effective a manager you are, it's inevitable that one or more of your employees will display problematic behaviors now and then. A top performer starts exhibiting less-than-stellar performance. A previously reliable employee is increasingly absent from work. A direct report arrives chronically late to important meetings.

Left unaddressed, these and other behaviors can hamstring your team's productivity as well as sap morale. How to combat problem behavior? This section offers numerous recommendations for restoring order and drawing a clear line between acceptable and unacceptable behavior in your team.

Step in Quickly When an MVP Goes off Track
By Margaret Butteriss and William Roiter

Not only do your most valuable players (MVPs) thrive in a favorable work environment, they're very sensitive to any deterioration in that environment. So, think of your MVPs as canaries in the mine shaft that react to a gas leak before the miners do. They're your early warning that trouble is brewing. And it's your job to figure out just what kind of trouble you're dealing with and what action to take. What do you do when your MVP begins exhibiting less-than-stellar performance? Start with these three tips:

- MVPs, by nature, question the status quo. They are constantly looking for ways to improve products, processes and people. Is a current disruption in performance due to colleagues who feel threatened by the MVP's questions or behavior? If the MVP is facing resistance in the face of improvement, tell the MVP about any problems being encountered and work with him to overcome resistance. If it is the MVP's behaviors that are disruptive and causing problems, let the MVP know as soon as possible. Then work with the MVP to take responsibility for the problems and find a way to resolve any open issues.

- Is there a prior history to the problems and any resolution? If so, you'll be able to talk with the MVP about the linkage and discuss what was learned previously. If you're a relatively new manager of this MVP, seek out institutional memory by checking with HR to learn what they know and recommend, talking with the previous manager or consulting your boss if she previously worked with the MVP.

- Has something dramatic changed for the MVP at work or outside of work? To successfully manage an MVP over time, a manager knows what an MVP does to succeed and also knows who the MVP is as a person. MVPs value personal connections with their cohorts, and these connections can be the foundation of a thoughtful MVP "catch."

When you're ready to talk to your MVP, be sure to discuss observed behaviors, not opinions. If you make a comment such as "You're pretty angry at Paul," the MVP can simply respond, "No, I'm not. I'm happy with Paul." Opinions can lead to fruitless arguments. Instead, focus on behavior. For example, you could say, "In our morning meeting, you told Paul that he was undermining your authority with your people and he had better stop it. I don't know if you saw this, but Paul and his direct report looked surprised and confused by this. Later, I took Paul aside and he told me that he had been responding to questions from your people." It's difficult to argue with this recitation of an observed behavior. And, at that point, you could remind the MVP that meetings are not the place to air a grievance and ask why the MVP's people are going to others for answers.

Also be sure to assess what's going on with the MVP. Has business alignment changed to self-interest? Has opportunity morphed into entitlement? Has developing others solidified into exaggerated self-importance? In other words, has the person lost the MVP's characteristics? If so, he needs to know that what once made him indispensable has slipped away and that you want to work with him to regain that effective edge.

You'll also want to be aware of any problems that the MVP is experiencing. The MVPs we interviewed identified four problems that could sour them on a good business:

- They are in the wrong job. One MVP who was a great salesperson had been asked to take over the sales manager job. Everyone thought she was doing her usual terrific job, except for her. She maintained high standards for herself and felt she wasn't meeting her standards. She was new to feeling like a failure and didn't like it one bit. She spoke up, and her manager listened to her. She was successfully moved to manage account executives and took over sales training.

- They get no respect. Something changes, and MVPs no longer feel they are important to the business. Their ideas aren't welcomed, and they don't feel they're a part of the decision-making process in their area of expertise. Don't confuse the MVP's need to be involved with a belief of entitlement. It is simply a feeling that their current contributions are no longer valued. The No. 1 reason MVPs leave a company or fail is a boss who has poor management skills and who does not value the MVP.

- They disagree with the company's vision. A change in strategy or direction is made that sidelines the MVP's goals, and no one has taken the time to talk with the MVP about new opportunities.

- The MVP has changed, and the business has not. Development plans may have been sidelined or abandoned. MVPs desire challenge; they want to contribute to the organization's success.

Our research about fallen MVPs also led us to another conclusion: If an MVP's performance falls, it is best to fix it quickly or, if it can't be fixed, come down hard on the MVP. The reasoning? It's just as important to demonstrate how to manage negative examples as it is to manage positive ones. One company president went so far as to say that he comes down harder on his best people because he and the other employees look to the MVP for leadership.

The biggest mistake you can make? Avoiding the problem and hoping it will go away. These employees have proven their value and their commitment to the business, and they have earned the opportunity to improve. While it may cost you and your company both time and money, with a little effort you should be able to recover one of your most valuable assets.

Absenteeism: Enforce the Rules without Legal Hassles
By Paul Falcone

It's not only frustrating when staffers abuse the absenteeism policy, it's costly—to the tune of about $600 per employee annually, according to estimates.

Yet many managers shy away from enforcing attendance rules because they fear legal liability under the Family and Medical Leave Act (FMLA) or the Americans with Disabilities Act (ADA). While these federal laws are complicated, they don't require you to tolerate excessive absenteeism. To counter absenteeism, your best defense lies in a well-crafted policy, consistent past practices and progressive discipline.

First, you'll need to know the details of your company policy. If there is no written policy, ask for one. The written policy is the guideline for determining excessive absenteeism. Juries typically consider one sick day per month, or 12 days a year, as a threshold. More than that and it's likely that any discharge would be sustained, but a plaintiff's attorney may convince a jury that your decision to terminate was premature if total annual absences are fewer.

Determine whether absences are measured in days or incidents (defined as an uninterrupted series of days for the same sickness or injury.) Are absences calculated on a rolling year or a calendar year? Does the policy require medical notes for employees to receive pay for sick time off? Some employers require doctors' notes once a certain threshold of incidents has been met, such as requiring notes for all occurrences beyond a fifth absence.

Beyond the nuts and bolts of the written policy, consistency in applying the policy is crucial. Examine your own past practices as well as those of the organization. If employers are inconsistent in applying the rules, judges and arbitrators often make them pay for their fickleness. If you find that your own past practice—or the organization's—has deviated from the written policy, ask advice from your HR professionals about how to get things back on track. By notifying employees in advance and in writing, you can change a policy or practice.

To deal with a specific problem, you must document it. Documentation should include the following:

- **Restatement of the policy.** Example: "Maintaining good attendance is a condition of employment and an essential function of your job. To minimize hardships that may result from illness or injury, our company provides paid sick time benefits. However, periodic sick leave taken on a repeated basis may be viewed as abuse of the system. It is your responsibility to establish legitimate illness or injury to receive sick leave pay."

- **Dates and days of the week of absences.**

- **Any negative impact of the absence.** Example: "The number of incidents has disrupted the workflow in our unit and has caused the department to incur unscheduled overtime because others have had to carry the extra workload. In addition, a temporary worker had to be assigned to your area so that the deadline for the project could be met."

- **Any patterns in absenteeism.** Example: "Our company defines a pattern as a frequent, predictable and observable employee action that repeats itself over time. All five of your occurrences were taken off around your regularly scheduled weekends and holidays. This 'patterning,' therefore, violates our organization's absenteeism policy."

- **Your organization's expectations,** along with a copy of the policy, if applicable, and the consequences of inaction. Example: "Janet, I expect you to immediately improve your attendance by minimizing any future occurrences of unscheduled, unauthorized absences. A copy of our attendance policy is attached. Please read it thoroughly today and meet with me tomorrow morning if you have any questions. If you meet these performance goals, no further disciplinary action will be taken. In addition, you will develop a greater sense of accomplishment in helping our department meet its production goals while minimizing staff rescheduling and last-minute overtime costs. Please understand, however, that failure to provide immediate and sustained improvement may result in further disciplinary action up to and including dismissal."

Where do FMLA and ADA come in? FMLA-related leaves usually center on episodic or chronic conditions that require inpatient hospital stays, continuing treatment by a health care provider or a period of incapacity of more than three calendar days. Usually employees who take sick time do not necessarily meet the threshold of having a "serious health condition," which means that FMLA may have little impact on your decision to document excessive absenteeism.

But doctors' notes that substantiate a "serious health condition" may preclude you from taking any adverse action because medical certifications need not identify the condition being treated unless the employee consents. To determine if an FMLA-qualified "serious medical condition" is involved, talk to legal counsel.

Excessive absenteeism and the ADA have a critical connection that works to your advantage. The ADA only protects a "qualified individual with a disability" who can perform the essential functions of the job either with or without a reasonable accommodation. Several courts have held that an employer cannot accommodate unpredictable or sporadic absenteeism.

The exception: situations in which employees could perform most job functions from home.

Also, you are required only to accommodate known disabilities. Don't ask employees about what's ailing them or you run the risk of accommodation. If you suspect a problem with ADA, again, consult legal counsel.

Excessive absenteeism is a symptom of a problem, the employee's refusal to hold himself accountable to report to work regularly. Before beginning progressive discipline, talk with the employee one-on-one. Explain the critical nature of the situation, ask what he would do if he were you and then ask for a verbal commitment that the problem will be minimized.

Your Absenteeism-Abuse Worksheet

One of your employees has been increasingly absent from work. Assuming the absences are not because of a serious health condition covered by the FMLA or ADA, you need to address the problem. Use this worksheet to document important information about the situation and use the information to correct the behavior.

1. What is your company's absenteeism policy? Write it here.

2. What dates and days of the week has the employee been absent?

3. What patterns do you see in the dates and days of the week you've listed?

4. How has the person's absenteeism affected your team's work and productivity?

5. What, specifically, do you expect the person to do to demonstrate that he or she is no longer abusing your organization's absenteeism policy?

6. What will happen if the employee corrects the behavior?

7. What will happen if he or she fails to correct the behavior?

Missing in Action: Handling Job Abandonment
By Martha Frase-Blunt

It's enough to make a supervisor weep. Why would an essential employee simply fail to turn up for work—for a day, or two or more? But, the more important question is, What should you do when you think an employee has abandoned his job?

"Job abandonment is probably more common these days because the economy has been so strong, and workers have a lot of options, especially young people in entry-level, unskilled or service positions," says Greg Kult, an attorney and shareholder with Hall, Render, Killian, Heath and Lyman in Indianapolis. "Job-switching has become so prevalent and casual that, in an employee's mind, it may seem inconsequential simply to leave without giving notice."

Employers differ wildly on how long they will cool their heels before enacting a separation. But employment policy experts are coming to consensus on a three-day stipulation. "Three days is safe," says Ethan Winning, employee relations consultant and author of *Labor Pains: Employer and Employee Rights and Obligations* (E.A. Winning & Associates, 2001; www.ewin. com.) "Two days is not enough, and four days is a lifetime." And many states, such as California and Maine, have case-law precedents on the books supporting the three-day stipulation.

Three days allows sufficient time for a missing employee who has been hospitalized, incarcerated or stranded without a phone to contact someone. And three days also allows time to investigate the absence. For example, in many cases, the missing employee may indeed have made contact with the organization but not with the appropriate supervisor. A co-worker, receptionist or line manager may have received the message but failed to pass it up the chain.

Determining whether the absence is related to any medical problem also is important because it could create a problem in regard to the Family and Medical Leave Act (FMLA). "If the employee's absence is suspected to be medically related in any way, the employer must investigate," says Chris Hoffman, a labor attorney with Fisher & Phillips in San Diego.

Consider the scenario of the employee who goes missing after telling his supervisor of a doctor's appointment. "Under Department of Labor regulations, the employer should be spending those three days trying to find out what's going on because the company arguably had notice of the employee's medical status," Hoffman explains. If the absence is medically related, FMLA kicks in, and the employee cannot be terminated as a no-show.

The Americans with Disabilities Act (ADA) also may pose a problem in regard to job abandonment. In the case of an employee with a history of psychiatric illness, periodic unexplained absences may be part of the drill. "An unscheduled leave of absence can be considered a reasonable accommodation [under these circumstances]," says Hoffman.

Hoffman cautions that even if you know for a fact that a no-show employee is working somewhere else, you shouldn't assume the separation will be uncomplicated by FMLA issues. "Say a worker had a job in your warehouse and developed back problems. He leaves without notice and begins working a clerical job elsewhere. An employer can still be subject to discrimination charges for terminating him for job abandonment."

Maternity leaves that end in a no-show can be particularly problematic, as they may involve both the FMLA and the ADA. Questions of what constitutes family leave or disability leave can become extremely complicated, and the onus is on the employer to sort it all out. Consider the case of Dintino v. Doubletree Hotels Corp., No. Civ. A., 96-7772, 1997 (E.D. Pa., 1997).

Audrey Dintino, Doubletree's manager of telemarketing, notified management that she would be taking a maternity leave of absence from July 15, 1994, through Oct. 17, 1994. But, in late June, pregnancy complications required her to take an immediate medical leave of absence. Believing her absence was now classified under unpaid medical leave/disability, she informed her employer that she would take her 12 weeks of FMLA leave after the expiration of the medical leave. She restated this again in a letter dated Oct. 7. She received no response and Doubletree discharged her on Nov. 28 for failing to return to work.

Dintino sued and won. The court claimed, "In all circumstances, it is the employer's responsibility to designate leave, paid or unpaid, as FMLA-qualifying, based on information provided by the employee." In essence, the burden is on the employer to notify the employee in writing as to how the absence will be qualified.

The lesson, says Kult, is to "proceed with caution on job abandonment. It can take two to three years to try a case, and if you lose, you can be looking at paying years of back wages—with interest." Also, don't assume you can terminate an employee for abandonment without exploring the labor issues. "Labor relations considerations are too often overlooked when the workplace is not a union environment," he adds.

But in the vast majority of cases, a no-show employee is truly surrendering the job. In terms of the employer's obligations, it's up to managers to inform HR, which needs to investigate the whereabouts of the employee to rule out a medical cause for the absence. In some cases, an employer searching for an AWOL employee may be the first to discover that the person is missing and may be in a life-threatening situation.

Once satisfied that the job has been abandoned, managers should create documentation for the employee's file showing that a change in status has occurred and on what date. Hoffman also recommends sending a registered letter to the employee identifying the action the company has taken and why. "The return receipt from the letter goes into the file, and there can be no dispute that the employee was informed. But usually you won't get a direct response." He also suggests including notes from the supervisor or others detailing attempts to contact the missing person.

For those employees who might be in a position to cry wrongful termination, Hoffman suggests leaving some wiggle room. "Even if you have someone who has fallen off the map for three days, but you can't rule out a medical condition, send a registered letter. But consider tacking on a sentence such as, 'If there is anything that would change our understanding of your absence, please contact us immediately so that we can re-evaluate your resignation as appropriate.'

"You are building in your 'out' because you never know when you're going to be challenged."

Don't Tolerate Outrageous Behavior
By Linda Wasmer Andrews

Outrageously egregious conduct frequently carries a steep price tag for employers—and managers. At times, companies even may be hit with punitive damages, which are intended both to punish the company and to deter others from similar conduct. In such cases, the legal damages alone can soar into the millions. But even when no legal action is taken, extreme misbehavior can poison morale—decreasing productivity, increasing absenteeism and turnover, driving up health care costs for stressed-out employees and generally dragging down the company's bottom line.

The targets of abuse aren't the only ones who suffer. Co-workers may become stressed-out, too. "Employees who observe or hear about harassment that goes unchallenged may feel anxious, fearing that they will be next; or depressed, feeling like the organization doesn't care about its employees," says Kathleen Rospenda, a psychology professor at the University of Illinois at Chicago. But it doesn't have to be this way. The sooner you spot the warning signs of egregious behavior, the better your chances of being able to stop it before it starts.

Mistreatment at the hands of co-workers or supervisors is nothing new, of course. Certainly, the lecherous male boss who can't keep his eyes and hands off the female staff has been around for centuries. Other prime targets for harassers and abusers may shift with the political winds. In today's workplace, be on the alert—and ready to take action—if your employees are targeting these new groups of harassment victims:

1. **"Homosexual" victims.** In many workplaces, the harshest abuse is reserved for individuals who are perceived as homosexual—regardless of whether they are or are not. The majority of such cases seem to involve male-on-male harassment, says Dale Carpenter, an associate professor at the University of Minnesota Law School who specializes in sexual orientation issues. Carpenter also believes that such male-on-male harassment is often more severe than other types. "There's typically more physical intimidation and more relentless teasing involved," Carpenter says. He recommends watching for teasing that is based on "an individual's failure to conform to gender expectations, such as calling a man a 'sissy.' That's a warning signal that an illegal environment of harassment may be in the process of being created."

2. **Teenage victims.** A spate of recent lawsuits has involved teenage plaintiffs, some of them young girls who were groped, asked for lap dances or even raped. In some cases, young workers are the victims of egregious abuse by other young employees. In such cases, lack of work experience could be a factor, says Naomi Earp, vice chair at the Equal Employment Opportunity Commission (EEOC). "If you have a 16- or 17-year-old worker with an 18- or 19-year-old supervisor, it could be argued that both the employee and the manager are relatively new to the workplace and may not fully understand the rules of behavior there," she explains.

3. **Muslim victims.** Since Sept. 11, 2001, much of the religion-based harassment has been directed at Muslims, and it's a trend that shows no sign of abating soon. For example, Linda Ordonio-Dixon, a senior trial attorney at the EEOC's San Francisco District Office, worked on a case in which four Pakistani Muslim workers at a California steel plant alleged they were ridiculed during their daily prayers, mocked for their traditional dress and called names. "The harassment went on for a number of years, it was conducted in concert with the supervisors, and there was a significant amount of emotional distress experienced by the

claimants," says Ordonio-Dixon. The result: a $1.1 million settlement. The lesson: Don't ignore fundamental anti-harassment policies and procedures.

When confronted with their bad behavior, the worst harassers and abusers often claim they either didn't realize it was unwelcome or had intended it as a joke. "Lisa" says that was the case with her former boss, the editorial director at a professional association who claimed she was joking when she made repeated comments comparing Lisa to a prostitute and a "slut." But that explanation didn't fly, says Lisa, when the editorial director continued making the comments after Lisa complained.

The implication is that many chronic offenders may not be entirely feigning ignorance about the havoc they wreak. When confronting such individuals, you may need to spell out the problem in very clear, concrete terms. And the sooner you get involved, the better your chances of preventing a relatively minor incident from spiraling into something much more sinister and destructive.

Beware of Those Who Bully Bosses
By Kathy Gurchiek

Do you think of bosses when you think of bullying? Think again. A substantial number of subordinates bully their bosses through repeated nonphysical, health-impairing psychological mistreatment that falls outside discriminatory harassment. And bullying is more prevalent than sexual harassment and racial discrimination, according to the Washington State-based Workplace Bullying and Trauma Institute.

The institute's web site identifies four bully types:

1. The fist-pounding, apoplectic person with the "screaming meemies" instills fear in not only the target but also any witnesses so they will be too fearful to respond.

2. The two-headed snake is friendly to the target but destroys the target's reputation behind the scenes. This is the most common type of bully—and may even be your lunch buddy.

3. The constant critic chips away at the target's confidence behind closed doors to ensure deniability of what was said.

4. The gatekeeper finds out what the target requires to perform his or her job, then wields control by withholding what is needed. This is the type most often associated with bullying a boss.

Bullying typically involves a target who is new—new to the job, new to the group, new to the role—says Gary Namie, cofounder of the institute. New managers set themselves up when they come in and say, "This is how I did it at the last job," because they challenge the status quo. One supervisor's life was made miserable by an older, subordinate female employee who saw the higher-ranking woman as a threat, Namie says. The subordinate refused to follow the supervisor's instructions, issued counter-instructions to the staff and created a reign of terror in the nonunion shop. The bully used her protected status as a minority to thwart disciplinary action from higher-ups by threatening litigation, Namie says, and more than once she received hefty settlements despite a reputation for creating supervisor turnover.

While "bullying up the ladder" often is hard to define and difficult to solve, bullying requires two conditions—it is rewarded and promoted, and the perpetrator rarely suffers negative consequences, says Namie. That's why clamping down on bullying requires senior management's active support.

A supervisor at least two levels above the targeted boss should be responsible for confronting the bully because bullies "respond to power and they respond to organizational pressure," says Namie. The high-level supervisor must make it clear this behavior will not be tolerated, must warn the person that the organization will monitor his or her actions and must put the bully on notice that termination will ensue if the behavior continues. Monitoring should continue for up to a year, he adds.

"You close the loopholes because these people are loophole experts," Namie says. "You either want them to change their conduct ... or leave."

Cope Creatively with the Punctually Challenged
By Diana DeLonzor

President Bill Clinton, actor Robert Redford and model Naomi Campbell are all reputed members of the better-late-than-never club—one that covers up to 20 percent of the U.S. population. If your employees are card-carrying members, they're also dragging down the business. Tardiness costs U.S. businesses more than $3 billion each year in lost productivity. The effect on the bottom line of the average business is significant, and adding to the total cost is the ripple effect of late-starting meetings, as productivity is affected throughout an entire organization.

Most chronically late people aren't purposefully tardy but tend to have difficulty with time management. In a San Francisco State University study investigating chronic lateness and its causes, we found that the punctually challenged often shared certain common personality characteristics such as anxiety, a penchant for thrill-seeking or low levels of self-control. Chronically late subjects also reported greater procrastination tendencies in general compared to the timely subjects.

A combination of prevention, penalties, rewards and coaching is often key to dealing with tardiness on an organizational level. The following steps can turn a chronically late workforce into a group of right-on-timers.

1. Discourage late-starting meetings. Send an e-mail reminder a half-hour before every meeting asking participants to be on time, or set one up in a computer calendar. Two minutes after the scheduled start time, close

the door. Then tackle the most important topics first. Open the door for latecomers, but do not backtrack to fill them in on missed discussions.

2. Establish a system of rewards for employees with perfect attendance and punctuality. Rewards not only act as an incentive to employees, they also serve as a reminder that punctuality is an important part of company culture. Punctuality incentives are often packaged with attendance records, and rewards can come in the form of anything from free employee parking to department store gift certificates.

3. Deal with lateness on an individual level. Although termination is always an option for employees with excessive tardiness, sometimes an otherwise wonderful employee simply needs a nudge in the right direction. Arrange a meeting with the employee to outline company policies and inquire about extenuating circumstances or logistical problems. Set clear, measurable goals for the future and clarify the consequences for being late. Document your conversation in writing and keep written documentation of future incidents. During the initial meeting, schedule a follow-up appointment to review the employee's progress. Scheduling a follow-up meeting helps reinforce to the employee that you are serious about the progress you expect and that you will be monitoring the situation over time.

What if your boss is the guilty party? If broaching the subject with your manager is too daunting, try enlisting the help of his assistant. Make it a habit to provide a copy of the agenda prior to each meeting and request help in getting the manager to arrive on time.

You also may want to approach the HR manager and mention that lateness is becoming a problem in general. Mention that you've noticed company culture beginning to lag in regard to attendance and punctuality, and that you think productivity may be suffering as a result.

If you're the one with the tardiness problem, here are steps to change your ways:

1. **Relearn to tell time.** Most late people consistently underestimate the time necessary to accomplish everyday tasks. This kind of "magical thinking" is the unshakable belief that you can drive the 10 miles to work in seven minutes flat, even if day after day you fail to do so. To avoid magical thinking, keep track for one week of how long your daily tasks actually take, then post those new time frames somewhere you'll see them every day.

2. **Banish your "just-in-time" mentality.** Late people tend to embrace the entrenched belief that it doesn't make sense to do anything until it absolutely must be done. To eliminate this just-in-time mentality, start doing things early. Every morning for one month, write down one task you'll do early that day—turn in a report before it's due, fill up your gas tank before it's empty or go to the ATM while you still have money in your wallet.

3. **Plan to arrive early.** Late folks tend to have an aversion to waiting, so they try to time their arrivals to the minute. This kind of split-second time management rarely works out. Always plan to be 15 minutes early and you'll probably make it just in time.

4. **Schedule your time.** Each morning, using the new time estimates you created when you relearned how to tell time, make a schedule of your daily activities with start and end times next to each item. Having a written plan helps you to see tangibly what you have time to do.

And if these tricks work for you, share them with your punctually challenged employees.

Did You Know?

- Up to 20 percent of the U.S. population is chronically late.

- Tardiness costs U.S. businesses more than $3 billion each year in lost productivity.

- Most chronically late people aren't tardy on purpose.

- Chronic lateness may stem from anxiety, a penchant for thrill-seeking or low levels of self-control.

- Chronic tardiness can be cured.

Don't Get Caught in the Legal Wringer When Dealing with Difficult-to-Manage Employees
By Robin E. Shea

Retaliation is one of the hottest areas of employment litigation. More than 27 percent of all charges filed with the EEOC in 2001 were retaliation charges. Unfortunately—and probably not coincidentally—retaliation claims also are among the hardest for employers to prevent.

Dealing with an employee who has engaged in protected activity and also has attitude or performance problems can be one of the biggest challenges facing even experienced, seasoned managers. In legalese, unlawful retaliation exists when three things happen:

1. An employee engages in legally protected activity.

2. The employee suffers an adverse employment action.

3. "A causal nexus" exists between the protected activity and the adverse action.

In plain English, this means that:

1. Your employee either tried to blow the whistle on your company for doing something he perceived to be illegal, or he filed an EEOC charge, a workers' compensation claim, a safety complaint or a lawsuit against the company.

2. You fired, demoted, failed to promote or cut the pay of that employee.

3. You took your actions in step No. 2 because of what the employee did in step No. 1.

There are two main reasons why retaliation claims form such a large chunk of all employment litigation. First, an inordinate number of people are entitled to file these claims because there are so many activities that are "legally protected." These include race or other discrimination charges, disability accommodation requests, requests for leave under the federal Family and Medical Leave Act, workers' compensation claims, workplace safety complaints, sexual or other harassment complaints and wage and hour complaints.

Most federal and state employment laws contain anti-retaliation provisions. The laws protect charging or complaining parties as well as those who testify on their behalf. As long as these individuals act in good faith, they are protected—whether or not they are actually right. Many of these laws also protect former employees. For example, an employer who gives a bad reference for an ex-employee because that person filed a charge could be liable for retaliation.

The second reason for the large number of retaliation claims is the difficulty employers have in dealing with people who have engaged in these types of activities. It is hard to be constructive in all of your dealings with an employee who has filed a charge against your company or against you personally.

To complicate matters further, the employees who engage in protected activity often (but not always) are your chronic complainers, gripers and "troublemakers." It is human nature to have trouble dealing with such individuals, yet anti-retaliation laws require almost superhuman restraint.

On the theory that understanding a problem is the first step in overcoming it, let's look at the dynamics in a fictional but typical retaliation scenario:

Protected activity. Seymour, a mediocre employee, files an EEOC charge of sex discrimination after co-worker Glenda beats him out for a promotion. Seymour alleges that Glenda got the promotion because she was sleeping with the boss. Although Seymour honestly believes this "must" be the reason he lost the promotion, he has no evidence to support the claim. The EEOC advises Seymour that his employer cannot take action against him for filing this charge. Seymour brags to his co-workers about the charge and says he is making things "very uncomfortable" for Glenda.

Anger/fear of inspiring new protected activity. Seymour's co-workers, in turn, begin to feel uncomfortable around him. Because he was willing to file a charge against the company, they reason, he might file a charge or make embarrassing allegations against one of them. They also believe he has been unfair to Glenda. Glenda, for her part, is aware of the charge and worries about the impact it may have on her career. She also is afraid to do anything that might bring on additional charges from Seymour. Finally, she is understandably hurt, embarrassed and angry at his allegations.

Avoidance. Glenda knows she cannot legally take any action against Seymour for making her life miserable. She can't be nice to Seymour because she is too angry with him, and she can't be mean to him because of the law. She is trapped—and so she makes her first mistake. She does the only thing a reasonable person in her position would do—she avoids him. She avoids personal contact with him, avoids giving him assignments and certainly avoids giving him constructive feedback about his performance and workplace behavior. Seymour's co-workers do likewise.

Pushing the boundaries. Although Seymour bristles a little at being avoided, he soon realizes he has it made. If he misses a deadline, Glenda asks a co-worker to finish the job. If he smarts off to Glenda or co-workers, they walk away. If he spends the workday shopping on e-Bay or talking to his lawyer about the lawsuit he intends to file against the company, they let it go. Because no one calls Seymour on his behavior, he begins pushing the boundaries even more.

Increased avoidance/excessive tolerance. The more he pushes, the more Glenda and his co-workers are intimidated and back away from him. They also tolerate increasingly poor performance and bad behavior on his part. Their tolerance spurs Seymour to push the boundaries even further, in turn causing more avoidance and tolerance and so on.

Resentment. Although Glenda and Seymour's co-workers appear calm and aloof on the surface, increasing rage is simmering below. They cannot repress their true feelings forever, no matter how much they try. The co-workers also begin to become impatient with Glenda, despite their sympathy for her, because they perceive that she is letting Seymour get away with murder.

The trigger. Seymour commits an infraction. It may be a relatively minor one, or one for which he has a legitimate explanation. In any event, because of the stress that has been building among Glenda and Seymour's co-workers, this infraction leads to ...

The explosion. (This stage also can be referred to as "being human.") Someone retaliates against Seymour. It could be a co-worker, or it could be Glenda. But the result is that Seymour is punished out of proportion to his actual offense, perhaps even being terminated for behavior that would result in no more than a warning if a co-worker had committed the same behavior.

There are also variants of the "disproportionate punishment" theme. Perhaps the co-workers harass or play a vindictive trick on Seymour while Glenda looks the other way. Or perhaps Seymour really does deserve to be fired, but because everyone was afraid to approach him until they became fed up, there is no supporting documentation in his file (thus, leaving the door open for him to allege that he was fired in a retaliatory manner).

This brings us back to the beginning of the cycle. Based on the "explosion," Seymour accuses the company of retaliating against him for filing his earlier sex discrimination complaint. And if the action was disproportionate, unduly cruel (at least, when viewed out of context) or insufficiently documented, he may have a good case.

The scariest aspect of the above scenario is that it could so easily happen to anyone. Managing an employee who has engaged in legally protected activity takes courage and resolve. But it can be done legally and correctly. Here's how to break the cycle.

The scenario above went wrong not when Seymour filed his charge, but when Glenda failed to deal honestly with his performance and attitude problems and chose instead to avoid him and tolerate his inappropriate behavior. Early on, Seymour did plenty to warrant disciplinary action: He missed deadlines, goofed off and was belligerent to co-workers. Glenda easily could have taken action against him for these infractions, consistent with company policy and practice.

It pays to remember that the law requires a "nexus" between the protected activity and the adverse employment action. In practical terms, that means that it is legal to take action against a protected employee for any reason other than a retaliatory one. What this means—and what we all have such a difficult time doing—is treating protected employees just like anyone else. We should give work assignments to an employee who has engaged in protected activity. We should hold that employee to the same standards as other employees. This is the only viable choice the law allows.

That doesn't mean it is an easy choice. In fact, it is incredibly difficult, given that the employee has already filed one charge against you and is likely to file another as soon as you confront him. However, there are two strategies that should make this task easier:

Let the employee's psychology work for you. It is very difficult for a person to continue working for a company against which he has filed a charge. Although it is hard for employers to keep a level head in such situations, it helps to know that the "protected" employee has his own set of challenges. Most agencies will advise the employee that he or she cannot be terminated for engaging in protected activity. But what many employees hear is, "You cannot be fired—period."

As a result, these employees often adopt a false sense of immunity that ultimately works to their disadvantage. They begin to do stupid things, including skipping work, refusing reasonable assignments, falsifying records, engaging in violent or verbally abusive altercations with supervisors or co-workers—in short, committing clear-cut, termination-on-first-offense infractions. Although it obviously would be wrong to terminate an employee for a retaliatory reason, the above types of infractions can and should be acted upon if they occur.

Examine your conscience. Retaliation cases normally stand or fall based on the manager's motivation. Thus, to make sure you're on solid legal ground, ask yourself the following questions before taking action against an employee who has engaged in protected activity:

• Is there a written attendance, behavioral or performance standard that the employee violated?

• What is the company's actual practice with respect to such violations?

• How would I treat my best employee if he or she violated this standard? (This one, answered honestly, is probably the key to assessing the purity of one's motives.)

• Is the proposed action supported by policy, practice and appropriate documentation?

- If the issue is a "gray" one (examples might include substandard performance or poor attitude), do you have sufficient, specific and objective data on which to rely?

Obviously, it also does not hurt to get an unbiased opinion from someone who has not been putting up with this employee for months, as you have.

Author's note: This article should not be construed as legal advice or as pertaining to specific factual situations.

Quick Tips for Addressing Problem Behavior in Your Team

- Is your top-performing employee suddenly exhibiting less-than-stellar performance? Identify and address the root of the problem: Consider whether he or she has been promoted into the wrong job, is feeling that his or her current contributions aren't valued, disagrees with the company's vision or needs more of a challenge.

- Do you suspect that one or more of your employees may be abusing your company's absenteeism policy? Counter the problem by ensuring that the policy is clear and that employees understand it, documenting patterns of absenteeism, and applying progressive discipline.

- Has an employee failed to show up for work in the past three days? If the extended absence is medically related, talk with your HR representative about possible FMLA and ADA considerations. Consult HR and an attorney to determine whether the person has surrendered his or her job. If so, work with HR and the attorney to document the change in status and to send a registered letter to the person identifying the action your company has taken, and why.

- Worried about employees' mistreating one another? Be especially alert to an increased tendency for employees to insult, mistreat or abuse homosexual, teenage or Muslim colleagues—the most common harassment victims today. Clearly communicate your company's anti-harassment policies, and promptly confront any abusers with their bad behavior.

- Do some of your employees arrive chronically late to meetings? Discourage late starts by closing the conference-room door two minutes after the designated start time and tackling the most important issues first. Open the door for latecomers, but don't backtrack to fill them in on missed discussions.

- Is one of your employees bullying you? Fist-pounding, back-stabbing, constant criticism and withholding information you need to do your job all constitute bullying behavior. Combat it by having a manager at least two levels above you in the organizational hierarchy confront the offender. Bullies respond to power and organizational pressure.

- Are you considering firing an employee for problem behavior? Before you do, make sure that the behavior in question doesn't constitute a legally protected activity—such as making harassment charges, asking for accommodation for a disability, requesting leave under the Family and Medical Leave Act or making a workers' compensation claim. Employees terminated for legally protected activities may charge your company with retaliation—leading to costly litigation.

SECTION SEVEN: MANAGING CONTINGENT WORKERS

In today's increasingly competitive business arena, many organizations look to contingent staffing to enhance their ability to respond flexibly to rapidly shifting conditions. Use of temporary workers, job sharing, and interns can provide your team with particularly valuable flexibility as well as other important advantages. Job sharing, for instance, enables many organizations to retain valued employees who want a part-time schedule. And hiring interns can help you "test drive" a potential candidate for a later full-time position.

The articles in this section identify the unique challenges associated with managing contingent workers, and provide helpful suggestions for getting the most from temporary workers, job sharers and interns.

To Make the Most of Your Temps, Manage Them
By Paul Morrow

Sooner or later, you're going to need a worker to fill in temporarily. By taking the time to provide careful instructions and orientation, you'll get much more out of your temps—and they'll get a favorable impression of your organization, which might be beneficial if you're hoping to recruit them eventually.

Here's a checklist to help you get started:

- How long will the job take? Unless there's a learning curve, keep in mind that temps do not have as much to distract them from the job at hand. Most likely, the temp will get the job done faster than you expect. Save time and money by planning for this.

- If the task for which you hired the temp is finished ahead of schedule, tell him he can go home. Why keep him around looking for something else to do just because you said you thought you needed someone for two weeks?

- Make sure the temp is oriented by introducing him to all personnel with whom he will be working and show him the location of supplies, equipment and lavatories.

- If a password is required, set up a temporary password that can be used by any temp you hire, such as "Temp1" or "Temp2," a phrase that can later be deleted and/or easily changed. Your human resources department might want to keep track of which temp is getting which password. If a security code is required for access to lavatories or elevators, provide him with an equally easy-to-delete code.

- Restrict instructions to the person who hired the temp. Don't allow other employees to give instructions that might be contradictory or confusing.

- Never leave a temp unattended in the office. Too often temps are left to fend for themselves, even on the very first day. These are the days when invariably something unexpected arises and the temp is forced to do his or her best, to no avail.

- If you really must leave a temp alone for any length of time, provide a phone number where you can be contacted.

To maximize use of a temp, provide careful and specific instructions, as much as possible in writing. Then, go over all procedures to avoid misunderstandings. Keep your instructions short and to the point; temps don't need or appreciate long, involved explanations of why things are done a certain way.

Once the temp is doing the job, avoid hovering; allow your written instructions to serve you. But if some task is time-sensitive, be sure to allow the temp to ask as many questions as he needs to do the job. Even if your written instructions have the answers, it might be quicker and easier for the temp to ask you.

For the first few days, keep in touch. Ask temps if they need anything, and find out how they are "settling in." Do what you can to let them know you are there to help them do a better job without micromanaging their work.

You'll also want to plan for "down time," which invariably occurs despite the most careful planning. You may be waiting for data from another office so the temp can enter it into the spreadsheet program. Or perhaps the temp has turned out to be very fast typist who has those letters all typed, envelopes printed and stamped and has carried everything to the mailroom.

In such cases, a dedicated, hard-working temp will ask, "What else can I do?" This could be a great opportunity for a temp who is being considered for permanent employment to find out more about your company.

Job-Sharing: It Has Benefits for Employees—and Employers
By Carolyn Hirschman

Over 16 years, Charlotte Schutzman and Sue Manix shared many jobs, survived two corporate mergers and a relocation—and earned two promotions. These days, they share the post of vice president of public affairs and communications at New York-based Verizon Communications Inc. They each work two days a week and on alternate Wednesdays and talk by phone at least twice a week. The advantage of their job-sharing arrangement? They've been able to stay on track professionally while raising their children. " If we didn't job-share," says Schutzman, "we might have left."

Experts agree that retaining skilled employees may be the major benefit of job sharing to employers. But job sharers also are more loyal, says Carol Sladek, a work/life consultant for Hewitt Associates in Lincolnshire, Ill. "People are very grateful for this kind of flexibility and are willing to go the extra mile," she says. And such loyalty can translate into better coverage and productivity than one full-time employee can provide. When a job-share partner is out sick or on vacation, the other partner may be able to step in. And job sharers typically schedule medical appointments and other personal business on their own time.

To work most effectively, job sharing requires the right match of job, job partners and manager. Although it can work for positions from administrative assistant to executive vice president, it works better with jobs that have specific duties and regular hours than with those involving less clearly defined tasks or substantial travel, experts advise. The best candidates for job sharing? Employees who are solid, committed performers and excellent communicators. And it helps if they are highly organized, compatible and willing to share successes and failures alike with their job-share partners.

For managers, job sharing isn't without challenges—especially in the additional oversight, increased administrative tasks and performance reviews for two employees rather than one. But first and foremost, managers must make the mental leap to accept—and support—the arrangement to have any chance of success. "It requires a leap of faith that the work will get done," says Tim Kane, Pittsburgh-based national leader of the virtual workplace solutions practice for Deloitte, the global consulting firm headquartered in Wilton, Conn.

It's also important to set specific performance expectations, determine how performance will be measured and check in with the partners regularly to see that things are on track. Specifics such as communication logistics can be made part of a job-share agreement, which some consultants say should be drawn up to help make the arrangement run smoothly. A written agreement, initiated by the partners and negotiated with their manager, should address performance expectations, details such as who's working when and other management concerns. There's no one answer to handle the logistics of job sharing, but partners and their managers should agree on the terms before the team starts work. Here are a few options:

- **Work schedules.** The job requirements, partners' preferences and office-space needs determine how to cover a 40-hour week. Some teams split five days, overlapping for a midweek lunch. Others divide a six-day week, with both working Wednesdays—technically, a 1.2 full-time equivalent. Another possibility is for each partner to work two days a week and to take turns working alternate Wednesdays. Some jobs can be split into two four-hour shifts every day. Whatever the schedule, try to keep it consistent so managers, co-workers and outside contacts know what to expect. Partners can cover for each other during vacations, maternity leaves and even sick days.

- **Compensation.** Some partners split a salary evenly in order to be treated as equals. Others receive half of what they were paid before becoming a job sharer so that their individual levels and experience are taken into account. If it's a combined six-day workweek, each partner is paid 60 percent of the salary in recognition of the 20 percent additional time spent on the job. For health and retirement benefits, follow the rules for part-time employees. Since two policies cost more than one, job sharers may pay the extra expense. Vacation and sick days can be split.

- **Performance evaluations.** These are subject to negotiation and policy. Some teams are evaluated together and then split any pay raise evenly. In other teams, partners are reviewed separately and get separate raises. Either way, the partners' ability to work as a team should be part of their evaluation criteria.

Your Job-Sharing Checklist

You're considering allowing two employees to share a job. And you want to be sure the arrangement delivers the promised benefits to your department. Check whether the following criteria for success will be met.

Criteria for job-sharing success	Yes	No
1. The position in question has specific duties and regular hours.	❏	❏
2. The job sharers are solid, committed performers.	❏	❏
3. The job sharers are excellent communicators.	❏	❏
4. The job sharers are highly organized and compatible.	❏	❏
5. The job sharers are willing to share successes and failures with each other.	❏	❏
6. You trust the job sharers to get their work done.	❏	❏
7. You've set specific performance expectations.	❏	❏
8. You've articulated how performance will be measured.	❏	❏
9. You've developed a written agreement specifying which partner will work when and how the partners will be compensated.	❏	❏

A Few Rules for Successful Internships
By Amy Maingault

With the summer internship season upon us, it's a good time to think about making the most of summer interns—but that doesn't mean palming off work that other employees are trying to avoid. Interns are looking for meaningful experience that is related to their field of study, and a successful internship program for both parties only occurs if you're willing to provide work that will look good on an intern's résumé.

Here are a few other tips to keep in mind:

• Consider carefully what qualifications you want your interns to have. To entrust an intern with meaningful work, you need to consider what kind of credentials the intern will need to perform. Specify whether an intern should have completed specific coursework or a certain number of years of college.

• Keep an eye on expenses. Although interns aren't usually as costly as regular employees, there are expenses involved. Recruiting can be costly, especially if you need to attend job fairs at various colleges.

• Be aware of the legalities. Most interns qualify as employees under various employment laws and are subject to minimum wage and overtime laws, workers' compensation coverage and possibly unemployment compensation. You may want to consult your HR staff to structure or revise benefit plans to exclude interns from benefits that aren't mandatory.

- Ensure ahead of time that office supplies, computer access and workspaces are available.

- Plan for time to supervise your interns. An intern is no solution to your work overload if you don't have the time and energy to oversee the work that a successful internship requires.

- Set aside time to provide ongoing feedback and to conduct a formal performance review.

- Ask your HR department for ongoing support. It's important that the HR department be available for interns who have encountered problems and for managers who are handling issues with interns.

You May Want to Hire Older Workers as Interns
By William Atkinson

Rethink your idea of intern candidates. Reason: More and more older workers are seeking internship positions, and their experience may give them a leg up on their competition. Mostly, these older workers are seeking positions to find a new direction for their careers, says a survey of more than 2,500 people by Right Management Consultants, a Philadelphia-based career transition firm. The survey found that while 56 percent were thinking of making a significant career change, those ages 56 to 60 were the most interested.

"Over the last 10 years, based on surveys we have done, we estimate a 10 percent or more increase in employers using older interns, and the trend toward companies using older interns is continuing to grow," says Mark Oldman, president of Vault Inc., a New York company that provides online career information and job listings. Vault's online resources are used by a lot of experienced workers who are interested in internships in the arts and entertainment field, Oldman says. Typically, they are people who started out in conventional jobs and then, after achieving some financial security, started looking for careers that they would find more creative and satisfying. "Investment banking isn't known for attracting older interns," Oldman says. "However, a lot of older investment bankers are interning in radio and TV stations, as well as newspapers and magazines."

For some, industry consolidations, such as banking and communications, are fueling the quest for change, says Doug Matthews, executive vice president at Right Management. In addition, many baby boomers are taking early retirement offers, which allow them to afford internships in fields they want to explore. And in a labor market where good candidates are hard to find, Matthews says employers are becoming more open to candidates from all demographic categories.

The internship program offered by the Smithsonian Institution in Washington, D.C., openly welcomes workers of all ages who take part in scientific or historical research, learn what is needed to become a museum professional or sharpen their administrative skills. Some work with political history collections and carry out library and archival tasks. Some interns come from museums or related fields, while others retired from former careers and decided to embark on new ones.

About 20 percent of the program's interns are older, and almost all are working on second careers, says Tracie Spinale, the institution's internship coordinator. Older interns, she says, often have a stronger sense of personal responsibility than younger interns and are not afraid to communicate their ideas or concerns. And they usually don't need much guidance. "They tend to be more proactive."

Harper's magazine in New York also hires experienced interns and uses its web site to welcome young interns as well as those who "use the program as an introduction to publishing after having pursued careers elsewhere." Benjamin Austen, the associate editor who also heads up the intern program, is a former English teacher who used *Harper's* internship program to break into publishing.

Older interns can provide perspective, seasoning and wisdom, says Oldman. "In some of these organizations, older interns serve as 'de facto' mentors," he adds. They also are likely to be comfortable in hierarchical environments, and they know how to get along with other people and build relationships that foster cooperation. Older interns also are more apt to view the experience as an integral part of a varied career, while younger workers may view the internship as merely a stepping-stone to another job.

One challenge for managers is that experienced interns who are used to having jobs requiring more responsibility may have expectations of greater responsibility than employers are willing or able to provide to an intern—at least until they prove themselves. "Managing [any] intern effectively involves guiding them in the early stages, then providing more responsibilities as they prove themselves," Oldman says. Spinale recommends managing the expectations of older interns up front. At the Smithsonian, project descriptions similar to job descriptions are created, and interns are told how their activities will fit into the overall project.

Managers who want to widen their pools of interns to include 30-somethings and beyond should look beyond traditional intern venues such as college web sites and spread the word through traditional advertising, online advertising, word of mouth, online HR bulletin boards and directories.

Did You Know ?

Older interns:
• Are often seeking to change direction in their careers.

• Frequently have a stronger sense of personal responsibility than younger interns.

• Aren't afraid to communicate their ideas or concerns

• Don't need much guidance.

• Provide perspective, seasoning and wisdom—serving as informal mentors.

• Feel comfortable in hierarchical environments.

• Know to get along with others and build relationships that foster cooperation.

• View their internship experience as an integral part of a varied career.

Use Internship Programs to Groom Strong Job Candidates
By Dawn S. Onley

Students often think of internships as a way to acquire professional skills—and a way to pay their bills. But savvy managers view their internship programs as a way to create a cadre of potential new hires with pertinent experience.

"Interns are a pipeline of full-time talent," says Steve Pollock, president of WetFeet Inc., a San Francisco-based research and consulting organization that specializes in talent recruiting. In fact, a student recruitment report released in July by WetFeet found that the average number of internship offers received by students at top-tier universities in 2005 jumped by 18 percent for undergraduates and 11 percent for MBAs, compared to 2004.

To kick your internship program into high gear, think beyond college fairs and campus career centers and consider sponsoring student groups, working with alumni associations and hiring on-campus representatives to identify potential interns. For example, Booz Allen Hamilton Inc., a consultancy based in McLean, Va., takes a targeted approach to its intern search by holding a series of career fairs and recruiting interns from 13 colleges and universities up and down the Mid-Atlantic region. The firm, which mostly draws technology and engineering students, also finds some interns through an employee referral program. In the summer of 2005, Booz Allen had 175 interns, up by 10 from the previous summer. The company usually makes offers to about 35 percent of its graduating interns.

Companies that are the most successful in recruiting interns start by setting the goals they hope to achieve from their internship programs, experts say.

Some of the decisions the company must make include deciding which area of the organization could benefit most from having additional staff, what organizational objectives—such as diversity or tackling a special project—can be furthered by the internship program and what the intern is expected to accomplish. You'll also need to prepare available staff to serve as mentors, communicate with interns on what is expected of them and make arrangements for physical considerations, such as a workstation or computer network permissions, office supplies and security access.

Most interns are usually put to work alongside full-time staff professionals. Making sure the intern has adequate supervision and that managers understand the demands of working with an intern are top priorities. In addition, training and orientation on issues such as the organization's rules on dress, behavior, ethics and technology use get interns up to speed quickly and ease their integration into the work environment. Equally important is a formal process to gather feedback about the intern's experience—and to provide a thorough critique of the student's work. At the end of the program, the intern and the company should complete a survey about the experience, like an exit interview. At Booz Allen, students receive a form at the conclusion of their internship in which they're asked to assess the program and to outline the work they performed.

The high value employers place on the work of interns is reflected in the fact that four out of five are paid for their efforts—often handsomely. WetFeet's study found the average salary offer for internships was $638 per week for undergraduates, with an average signing bonus of $302. This compares to a $1,473 average weekly salary for MBA students with an average signing bonus of $693.

Unpaid interns—about 20 percent of all interns, according to Pollock—typically earn college credit for their work. Organizations that have unpaid interns must adhere to the Fair Labor Standards Act (FLSA), a federal law that sets workplace standards on wage and overtime requirements, among other things. The Department of Labor has compiled a list of criteria to help employers determine whether a student intern is considered an employee within the meaning of the FLSA. In essence, the work being performed by an unpaid intern should be a part of the student's college curriculum and should primarily enhance the student's skill set in much the same way conducting college lab work does.

The Washington Center for Internships and Academic Seminars, an educational nonprofit that places student interns with thousands of organizations in government, business and the nonprofit sector in the Washington, D.C., area, enables students to earn up to a full semester of credit for their work.

While the rewards of a successful internship program can be great, not every temporary stint blossoms into a lasting relationship and, just as they do with regular employees, employers have to work at earning the stature of an employer of choice. Roughly 39 percent of all graduating seniors and 61 percent of MBA graduates received offers for full-time employment in 2005, usually from the companies where they worked as interns, according to the WetFeet study. But 51 percent of the students declined the offers, citing more often than not a better offer from another company. This suggests "either that students successfully parlayed their summer experience into a good résumé builder, or that internship employers were not great at providing a compelling reason for their interns to convert," the WetFeet study found.

Did You Know ?

- The average number of internship offers received by students at top-tier universities in 2005 jumped by 18 percent for undergraduates and 11 percent for MBAs, compared to 2004.

- The average salary offer for internships in 2006 was $638 per week for undergraduates, with an average signing bonus of $302.

- About 20 percent of interns are unpaid.

- In 2005, 51 percent of graduates receiving offers of full-time jobs from previous internship employers turned down those offers—suggesting that employers need to provide more compelling reasons for interns to convert to full-time.

Quick Tips for Managing Contingent Workers

- Are you wondering how to get the most from temporary workers? Assume that they'll get the job done faster than you expected—and save time and money by planning for this. Provide specific, concise instructions. Don't let other employees give temps instructions; they may be contradictory or confusing.

- Are you considering letting two of your employees share a job? Make sure they're solid and committed performers, highly organized, willing to share successes and failures and excellent communicators.

- Want to extract maximum value from your summer interns? Don't forget to supervise them and provide ongoing feedback. Watch expenses—such as attending job fairs at various colleges. And specify the qualifications you want them to have—such as completion of specific coursework.

- Need mentors for your employees? Consider inviting older workers to serve as interns. They can provide perspective, seasoning and wisdom, serving as de facto mentors.

- Wondering how best to find summer interns? Look beyond college fairs and campus career centers. Sponsor student groups and work with alumni associations. Ask your current employees to suggest names.

SECTION EIGHT:
COMMUNICATING EFFECTIVELY

Your ability to communicate effectively with employees can make or break your career as a manager. Why? Through spoken and written communication, you accomplish vital managerial tasks such as conveying instructions, providing needed feedback and dealing with conflicts.

In this section, you'll find articles containing a wealth of recommendations for enhancing your communication skills. Ideas include adapting your communication style to the situation at hand, listening effectively and delivering painful news without triggering backlash.

Focus on Five Key Strategies to Improve Communication Skills
By Joelle Jay

Effective communication is one of the biggest factors in successful leadership. Without good communication skills, managers often fail to gain commitment from employees, achieve business goals and develop rapport with the people on their teams. In short, they can fail as leaders—no matter how good their intentions—if they fail to be good communicators. The good news? Managers can enhance their communication skills by committing to and practicing these five key strategies:

1. Listening.

2. Facilitating.

3. Questioning.

4. Using discretion.

5. Directing.

First and foremost, the most effective leaders know when to stop talking and start listening. This is especially important in three situations: when emotions are high, in team situations and when employees are sharing ideas. Extreme emotions, such as anger, resentment and excitement, warrant attention for both personal and business reasons. On a personal level, people feel acknowledged when others validate their feelings, and when managers ignore feelings, they create distance between themselves and their employees. From a business perspective, emotions can also interfere with clear thinking. Allowing employees to address their emotions helps them move beyond the situation at hand and get back to business. Managers can develop stronger relationships with their employees while enhancing productivity simply by listening to their employees when emotions are high.

Listening also is critical in team situations, which involve multiple personalities, complex dynamics and competing agendas. By listening carefully, managers can ensure that everyone is working toward the same goal. Listening also helps managers identify and address conflicts early, as well as facilitate healthy working relationships among team members. Third, listening is vital when employees are sharing ideas. When managers stop listening to ideas, employees stop offering them, and managers are essentially cut off from the creativity and expertise of the people on their teams.

The basic fundamentals of good listening include the following:

• Attending closely to what's being said, instead of focusing on what you want to say next.

• Allowing others to finish speaking before taking a turn.

• Repeating back what you've heard to give the speaker the opportunity to clarify the message.

Facilitating communication goes beyond listening; you're actually leading a conversation. Good facilitation consists of a continuous cycle of three steps: hearing what is said, integrating it into the topic at hand and saying something to move the conversation forward. For example, imagine a manager facilitating a meeting in which she and her team are developing goals for the coming year. The conversation might sound something like this:

Manager: As we develop our goals for next year, it's important that we hear from everyone in the department. What are your ideas?

Employee 1: I think it's important that we get productivity up. I notice we have a pretty relaxed pace around here, and it gets frustrating when some people are working hard and others seem to be contributing less than others.

Manager: OK, so we need improved productivity. What would that look like as a goal?

Employee 2: Actually, I think it's more a matter of setting a higher sales goal than improving productivity in the office. We don't just need to be busier, we need to get better results.

Manager: I see. So the idea is that we should set higher sales goals for everyone, which would consequently address the productivity issue. Is that right?

Employees: Yes.

Note that the manager repeated what she heard so that the employees could verify its accuracy. She also integrated each comment into the topic at hand—tying the first employee's frustration with productivity to the task—goal-setting—and connecting the second employee's point about sales to the topic on the table—productivity. Although her employees were providing the input, the manager stayed focused on the task of preparing goals and led all comments in that direction.

Good facilitation skills help managers become leaders because they are able to garner the input of everyone in a group while keeping them focused on the task. It's especially useful when guiding a team toward a desired outcome, such as developing a strategic plan, putting together a joint project or coordinating activities.

Questioning is how we get information, but it's important to remember that different kinds of questions yield different kinds of results. For example:

- Closed questions elicit yes/no answers. Use them when you simply need to check the status of an issue. Has the report been completed? Do you know what to do? Can you get that to me by Friday?

- Open questions elicit longer responses. Use them almost anytime you want more than a yes/no answer, such as seeking input from others, looking for information about a particular topic or exploring a problem. What do you think would be the best way to go about this? How are you doing on that project? What went wrong? These kinds of questions give others the chance to provide the information they have and to avoid the innumerable consequences that can come when leaders make assumptions without becoming well-informed.

- Personal questions have a special role in leadership. Inappropriate personal questions, such as asking direct reports if they are dating anyone, can alienate employees. Appropriate personal questions, however, can create a sense of camaraderie between employee and boss. Ask whether employees had a nice weekend, inquire about their families or follow up on common interests to connect on a personal level.

Knowing when not to speak as a leader is just as important as speaking. Managers must understand that the moment they don a new title, they become a leader—one who others look to for guidance, direction and even protection. Good leaders adopt a policy of discretion, if not confidentiality, with their employees. Only then can they develop the trust that is so vital to productivity. Confidential situations may arise in a number of areas, personal and professional, including the following:

- An employee involved in a direct conflict with another employee.

- An employee concerned about another employee's conduct.

- An employee's declining performance.

- An employee's health issue or personal problem.

- An employee's desire for advice on how to excel without being seen as cozying up to the boss.

In any of these cases, the employee is facing circumstances that affect him personally and could affect business if not addressed effectively. By inviting a confidential conversation, you could help your employee discuss a situation openly and develop strategies to handle it well. But if your trustworthiness is questionable, your employee won't believe a candid discussion is possible.

To communicate that you can be trusted, tell employees directly that you are always available for private conversations when needed. This further assures employees that the conversation will be kept confidential. Then keep that promise. Remember, actions speak louder than words. Employees doubt the discretion of managers who talk behind their employees' backs, gossip or show favoritism of any kind, which leads to communication shutdown.

Directing comes last on the list of communication strategies because it is the one strategy that should be used less often. Many managers direct their employees because they believe it's the only way to get things done. It's not. The other forms of communication discussed above—listening, facilitating, questioning, using discretion—are better able to get employees working more productively in a spirit of cooperation and in a more friendly environment than directing.

But directing has its place, when you want to give directions clearly and unequivocally so that employees know exactly what to do and when. It's best used in times of confusion or when efficiency is the most important goal. Although it can be effective, directing also can lead to complacency on the part of employees who may adopt an "I just do what they tell me" attitude. Use it sparingly.

Choosing the Right Communication Skill

Use . . .	If . . .
Listening—attending closely to what's being said, avoiding interrupting, paraphrasing what you've heard	• Emotions are running high. • You're communicating with a team. • Employees are sharing their ideas with you.
Facilitating—hearing what's said, integrating it into the topic at hand, moving the conversation forward	• You're leading an important conversation or meeting involving more than just a few participants.
Questioning—asking yes/no questions	• You need to check the status of an activity or task.
Questioning—asking open questions	• You want detailed information about a particular topic. • You're exploring a problem. • You're seeking input from others.
Questioning—asking appropriate personal questions	• You want to create a stronger sense of camaraderie in your group.
Saying nothing—respecting employees' confidentiality	• You want to respect confidences about appropriate personal matters, such as an employee's health or desire for advice on how to advance in his or her career.
Directing—giving instructions clearly and unequivocally	• Confusion reigns, and you want employees to know exactly what to do and when. • Efficiency is your most important goal.

Learn How to Listen Effectively to Enhance Employee Relationships
By Madelyn Burley-Allen

Listening is probably the most essential component of being a successful supervisor. Why? Because the one attribute most often stated about a well-liked boss is, "She really listens to me." That's especially important when your employee has a gripe.

Consider the following exchange between Bill and his supervisor, Dave:

Bill: "Dave, I'm really discouraged about the way things have been going on the job. It just never goes the way I expect it to. And, it seems like you're never around anymore."

Dave: "Sounds as though you've been doing quite a bit of thinking about this. Go ahead."

Bill: "Well, we are a week behind in production, and our supplies are not coming in on time. I feel swamped and unable to catch up. And, when I have tried to find you lately to see about getting some extra help down there, you are not available."

Dave: "Seems that you feel cut off from any support from me."

Dave's comments demonstrate not only that he is listening to what Bill has to say but that he cares about what Bill has to say. That kind of listening is learned; it doesn't happen automatically for most people. On average, people are only about 35 percent efficient as listeners. But by improving your listening skills, you can reduce the chances for misunderstandings, conflict, poor decision-making or a crisis because a problem wasn't identified in time.

Listening can be divided into three levels characterized by certain behaviors that affect listening efficiency. These levels are not sharply distinct; they're general categories into which people fall, and they may overlap or interchange, depending on what is happening. When people move from Level 3, "the least effective," to Level 1, "the most effective," they increase their potential to understand and retain what is said.

Level 1 listeners look for an area of interest in the speaker's message; they view it as an opportunity to gather new and useful information. They're also aware of their personal biases and attitudes and are better able to avoid making automatic judgments about the speaker and avoid being influenced by emotionally charged words. They strive to see things from another's point of view and avoid advocating a position. This listening behavior allows them to tap into their higher creative intelligence. Level 1 listeners also try to anticipate the speaker's next statement, to mentally summarize the stated message, question or evaluate what was said and to consciously notice nonverbal cues. Their overall focus is to listen with understanding and respect.

Level 2 listeners mainly listen to words and the content of what is being said, but they fail to understand the speaker. They forget that words don't communicate; it's the meaning and the understanding of words that creates effective communication. For example, Level 2 listeners zero in on words but, many times, they miss the intent because they neglect to pay attention to what is being expressed nonverbally through tone of voice, body posture, gestures, facial expression and eye movement. As a result, Level 2 listeners hear what the speaker says but make little effort to understand the speaker's intent. Obviously, this may lead to misunderstanding, incorrect actions, loss of time and a variety of negative feelings. In addition, because the listener appears to be listening by nodding his head in agreement and not asking clarifying questions, the speaker may be lulled into a false sense of being listened to and understood.

At Level 3, people tune out the speaker; they're either daydreaming, forming rebuttals, faking attention or are more interested in talking than listening. Once someone is finding fault, being judgmental or closed off, breakdowns in relationships and poor decision-making occur and the speaker or listener is more likely to move into the flight-or-fight mode.

To improve your listening skills, try to practice the following guidelines on a daily basis:

- Be attentive. Create a positive atmosphere through your nonverbal behavior by maintaining eye contact, an open relaxed posture, a friendly facial expression and a pleasant tone of voice. When you're alert, attentive and relaxed, others feel more important and more secure.

- Be interested in the speaker's needs and demonstrate your understanding and respect.

- Show a caring attitude. Allow the speaker to bounce ideas and feelings off of you while assuming a nonjudgmental, non-criticizing manner. And, don't ask a lot of questions right away, which can make someone feel as if he's being "grilled."

- Reflect back what you think the other person is feeling. Summarize what others say to make sure you understand what they're saying.

- Don't let the other person "hook you." This can happen when you get personally involved and usually results in anger and hurt feelings or motivates you to jump to conclusions and be judgmental.

- Use verbal cues. Acknowledge a speaker's statements using brief expressions such as, "Hmm," "Uh-huh," "I see," "Right" or "Interesting." Encourage the speaker to reveal more by saying, "Tell me about it," "Let's discuss it," "I'd like to hear what you're thinking" or "I'd be interested in what you have to say."

How Effectively Do You Listen?

Many of us may think we're listening far more effectively than we really are. To gauge your effectiveness as a listener, complete the checklist below. The more "Yes's" you check off, the stronger your listening skills.

When I'm listening to someone else, I...	Yes	No
1. View the exchange as an opportunity to gather new and useful information.	❏	❏
2. Notice my personal biases and avoid judging the speaker.	❏	❏
3. Avoid being influenced by emotionally charged words.	❏	❏
4. Try to see things from the other person's point of view.	❏	❏
5. Avoid advocating a position.	❏	❏
6. Seek to anticipate the speaker's next statement.	❏	❏
7. Mentally summarize what the other person has said.	❏	❏
8. Consciously notice the other person's nonverbal cues.	❏	❏
9. Maintain eye contact; an open, relaxed posture; and a pleasant expression and tone of voice.	❏	❏
10. Paraphrase the other person's statements so he or she can correct any misunderstandings.	❏	❏
11. Use verbal cues ("I see," "That's interesting") to acknowledge the other person's statements and move the conversation forward.	❏	❏

Be the Bearer of Bad News— Without Getting Burned
By Paul Falcone

Giving and receiving bad news is a common part of business; however, focusing on how to deliver bad news as well as ensuring that your subordinates are keeping you abreast of unpleasant changes in circumstances are critical in this information-driven work environment. A simple rule to share with your employees is this: Tell them: "I don't mind that bad news occasionally hits the fan; I simply want to know which way to duck when it does. You're responsible for communicating any problems to me before I learn about them from anyone else. There can be no exceptions while I'm at the helm."

Simple enough. But what about when you have to deliver bad news to CEOs and other senior executives who have a tendency to shoot the messenger? Unfortunately too many managers opt to take the path of least resistance by avoiding unpleasant confrontations with senior managers, even if this is to the detriment of the company. There's a better way. By using the following steps to deliver your news, you'll improve your chances of being heard—without endangering your career.

Step 1: Confirm your commitment to keep the enlightened CEO informed.

Every CEO relies on his immediate core of senior managers to remain abreast of changes in company circumstances and employee attitudes. When a member of senior management finds out about problems that were not communicated in advance, a tongue-lashing typically follows. The CEO never seems to acknowledge that the last time a manager brought bad news to his attention, he was pummeled and bloodied and became the hot topic of water cooler banter for a month. Let's say you're a regional business manager who's responsible for payroll and planning budgets and need to share some touchy information with your senior manager. You could begin like this:

"I have some information to share with you that might surprise you, and I'm not looking forward to this conversation, but that's why you pay me. I figure if I can't bring problematic issues to your attention, then I'm not doing my job. It's August, and I believe that we should plan to go over budget on our 'salaries and wages' line for the year. If you agree, I would need to upgrade the salary line on our Estimate 3 report by $33,300 to capture the variance that I'm proposing."

Step 2: Briefly outline the pros and cons of your proposal.

Here's one approach: "The good news is that we successfully navigated a number of unexpected challenges in the first three quarters, including four layoffs in our Seattle sales office, as well as the renegotiation of the Tacoma branch manager's contract. Paying out severance for those four employees as well as for that unexpected contract battle affected our wage line by $74,000. We were able to sustain that amount in our overhead budget because we allowed sufficient wiggle room in case of emergencies. The 'surprise' has to do with the fact that we need to put a retention program into place for some of our key players. Many of our people feel as if they're treading water in their careers and are looking to make up for lost time salary-wise. If we don't increase their base salaries in the fourth quarter, either by promoting them or implementing equity adjustments to bring their pay in line with competitor companies, then we'll lose them. We just don't have the bench strength to replace key players, and it's worth considering a budget overage to keep them in place."

Step 3: Overcome the CEO's initial objections pre-emptively, and do the math when focusing on the how.

Remember to tie the proposal needs to the bottom line—expenses. Any "lofty" proposals that haven't been logically thought out or financially justified will seem naïve at best and could result in your loss of credibility. Here's one way to phrase it:

"I know what you're thinking: We've responded logically to the recession by not back-filling open jobs and keeping payroll increases down by freezing promotions and equity adjustments. So why the change in strategy now? The bottom line is that we have identified 16 key players in total—six for promotion and 10 for equity adjustments—who will require $65,000 in payroll upgrades. We will only be able to permanently offset about half the variance using other budgeted headcount. Therefore, I'm recommending that we add an additional $33,300 to the 'wages' line to reflect the proposed upgrades for the Western region. Before we discuss the individuals in question, what are your initial thoughts?"

Regardless of the senior manager's ultimate decision, you'll have created a compelling presentation with a logical business conclusion. More important, you'll have couched the bad news in a contextual framework that forces your boss to consider your proposal on its objective merits, and you'll have fulfilled your responsibility of providing organizational insights that the senior manager may not have focused on. This is a well-done opener that will hopefully lead to further questions and investigation.

When it comes to working with your subordinates, creating a culture of trust is an amalgam of formal guidelines that you establish as well as informal, unspoken cues that you give. Of course, there are tools available to help you do this. For example, inviting your employees to evaluate themselves before you judge them during the annual performance review process allows them to involve themselves in their own career development, while placing you in the role of career mentor and coach rather than unilateral judge and decision-maker.

Similarly, adding a question to a one-on-one meeting with a subordinate would likewise help establish trust in your relationship, such as: "What could I do differently to provide you with more structure, direction and feedback or otherwise help you prepare for your next move in career progression?" If your subordinates believe it's safe to stick their necks out and share bad news with you, there's a greater chance that you'll hear about problems proactively while you can still fix them.

But what do you do if a subordinate stubbornly refuses to provide you with negative feedback? A written response may be an appropriate measure. Of course, we typically think of written responses in the form of progressive disciplinary written warnings, but written responses need not only appear in disciplinary warnings. Occasionally, a letter of clarification or a revised job description could achieve the same result without the negative sting attached to a warning. In any case, be sure that you clearly document your expectation that open communication, especially regarding potentially bad news, remains the subordinate's ultimate priority in all business dealings.

When it comes to obligations of sharing bad news, no lesson is more critical than dealing with requests for confidentiality from subordinates. Corporate managers often err on the side of protecting employees' privacy when their subordinates share improprieties in the workplace. That's a major mistake because a request for confidentiality can be used against the company in court.

What's the best way to handle this? Add a disclaimer to your management vocabulary, and tell employees who ask to speak with you in confidence that your ability to keep the information confidential depends on the nature of the issue. If it has to do with discrimination, harassment, potential violence in the workplace or any kind of conflict of interest, then you'll have an obligation to disclose that information to senior management. Otherwise, there's a good chance that you'll be able to protect the confidentiality request.

Seven Strategies for Being Seen as a Fair Boss
By Kelly Mollica

Fairness is all about perception. You may believe that you've been fair to your employees, but what really counts is that they perceive you as fair. Here's why:

A climate of real or perceived unfair treatment typically spawns negative attitudes and destructive behaviors, such as low commitment to the organization, distrust in management, job dissatisfaction, absenteeism, psychological stress, aggressive behavior, retaliation, theft and turnover. Clearly, all of these outcomes are damaging to employee morale and the organization's bottom line.

Your employees always expect you to be fair, but they tend to closely scrutinize for fairness in two key areas:

• When they receive unpleasant news, such as negative performance feedback, denial of a promotion or a lower-than-expected pay increase.

• When managers are implementing changes in policies and procedures, such as overtime calculations, work rules or reporting relationships. Your employees will naturally be concerned about how those changes will affect them, and they will be on the lookout for any evidence that the changes were handled unfairly.

It's particularly important to up your "fairness ante" at those times by heeding the following seven strategies:

1. Tell the truth.

Victor, a supervisor, expected a promotion to assistant manager. But his boss told him budget constraints prevented the promotion. Victor felt let down but didn't feel he had much to say if the company couldn't afford to promote him. The following month, when another supervisor, Anne, was promoted to the position Victor had sought, he was furious. Although he liked Anne and thought she was competent, he was angry because his boss had lied to him. From the grapevine, Victor learned he hadn't been promoted because his boss thought he "just wasn't ready yet."

Victor's boss erred in not telling the truth. Not only are you doing an employee a disservice by trying to soften the blow, failing to disclose information leads to perceptions of unfairness, says Don Herrmann, SPHR, director of human resources at Lake Hospital System in Painesville, Ohio. Employees deserve sincere and honest explanations about how the decision was made, who made it and what factors were considered, although not every detail of the decision is necessary.

2. Provide counseling.

To keep the conversation on a positive note, demonstrate your interest in the employee's success and offer resources when available. For example, in Victor's situation, his boss could have told him specifically what he needed to do to improve his chances for a promotion and encouraged him to sign up for training opportunities, take advantage of the company's tuition assistance or pursue other avenues of career development.

3. Be accurate.

Teresa, a customer service representative, was a little nervous when a larger competitor bought out her company. Still, she knew she was a valuable employee; she had the highest performance rating among her peers in her geographic region. Several weeks after the buyout, Teresa was bewildered when her new manager, Ben, told her she was being moved to accounts receivable. Ben hadn't even bothered to read her previous performance reviews.

When she insisted that Ben request her HR file and read her reviews, Ben begrudgingly agreed that Teresa's performance had been exemplary. But he stuck with his decision to transfer her. Teresa never again trusted Ben to look out for her best interests and, eventually, she left the company.

The lesson here? Make sure you base decisions on accurate information. If you aren't well informed about an employee's situation, take the time to learn the whole story. If performance is the criteria for granting pay raises and promotions, use recent, factual performance data. If it's obvious to the employee that you ignored her performance appraisals, or that performance was not documented, she will view your decisions as arbitrary. In some cases, if you suspect that performance information may be biased or inaccurate, postpone making a decision until more valid information about performance can be documented.

4. Pay attention to your bias.

Laura wanted to offer her 27 employees the option to work flexible schedules. She communicated the policy changes and met individually with employees to determine their schedule preferences. Laura, with three children at home, later realized that she had encouraged employees with children to take advantage of the flexible schedules, while subtly discouraging childless employees from doing the same. Laura immediately scheduled a meeting with all of her employees and apologized for the inconsistency, offering each employee the opportunity to submit a request to change their schedule preferences.

One way to prevent bias is to avoid making decisions in a vacuum. When appropriate, seek out other managers who can provide additional perspectives and ask for their honest opinions. Pay extra attention to colleagues who have a different "take" on the situation; they may help you keep an open mind. You also can try to put yourself in your employees' shoes. Ask yourself, "Is there anything about this situation that might suggest the possibility of favoritism?"

5. Be consistent.

When you use different sets of rules to judge people, employees will view your actions as capricious and untrustworthy. It's not uncommon for managers to "ignore" rules for certain employees or apply rules more rigidly to one over another. By doing this, you are virtually guaranteeing that your employees will see you not only as unfair but also unethical.

On the other hand, it's important to recognize that consistency needn't be rigid. Leave some room for common sense. For example, Herrmann described a situation in his organization where an employee who had outstanding attendance for several years suddenly missed several days of work. According to policy, the employee should have been written up and disciplined, but Herrmann encouraged the employee's manager to take the employee's individual situation into account rather than inflexibly adhering to policy.

6. Give employees 'voice.'

Ray, an engineer in a large construction firm, was surprised when his manager announced a new policy to assign projects among engineers. "You know," Ray grumbled to co-workers during lunch that day, "we could have come up with a better system for assigning work. They didn't even ask us what we thought." The other engineers nodded in agreement. From that day forward, productivity plummeted as the engineers frequently complained to managers that projects weren't distributed fairly. Months later, the policy was abandoned.

When possible, solicit employee viewpoints when you're planning major changes. Employees will be more likely to see their organization as fair and be committed to the outcome if they've had some "voice," or input, into rules and procedures that affect them.

7. Take corrective action.

Even after hearing your rationale, some employees may seek an impartial review of the decision through a formal grievance system. If they do, don't make them feel guilty or rebellious for seeking another assessment of the situation. If you felt that a decision made about you was unfair, you'd want the same opportunity for review. Give your employees the same treatment you'd expect yourself.

And if, during the formal review process, new data appear that support your employee's viewpoint, admit your error and correct your decision. Refusing to change a decision after you've received new data could be viewed as unfair. You may be afraid that changing your mind makes you look "soft" to your employees, or that you'll become an easy target for employees who don't like what they hear. On the contrary, employees will be grateful for your willingness to reverse a decision based on solid information, and perhaps, more importantly, they will respect and trust you when you insist on standing firm on future decisions.

Hone Your E-Mail Messaging Skills to Improve Communications
By Andrea C. Poe

E-mail is supposed to accelerate office communication—and it does. But the lack of interactivity and real-time communication also introduces problems. Just ask Marnie Puritz Stone. When she was an account executive at a Dallas-based public relations firm, nearly all intra-office communication was done via e-mail—no matter how sensitive. Her managers may have felt they were being efficient, but she and her colleagues thought the managers were rude. "I think that the callousness with which e-mail delivers news—good or bad—is a poor way to show leadership," she says. "And it creates a lot of resentment."

One problem is you can't create tone with e-mail, which increases the potential for misinterpretations. Disagreements that might have been cleared up quickly in face-to-face conversations often fester when the recipient misinterprets an e-mail message. Then, there's the lack of etiquette and standards, which also leads to communication snafus. "A lot of managers don't even bother to say please or thank you—or even sign their names," says Samantha Shepard, who works in the graphics department of a New York law firm. "That doesn't make you rush to do what they want."

The bottom line: There are real consequences of poor e-mail skills. "How you communicate with each other affects productivity, morale and retention," says Kenneth Pritchard, a human resource and management consultant in Lusby, Md.

So, how do you improve your e-mail messaging skills—and those of your employees? By setting an example for other employees in how you use e-mail, says Carol Beaudu, president of CJB Associates, a Seattle-based HR consulting firm specializing in technological issues. "A few niceties go a long way," says Perrin James Cunningham, president of Ethologie, a business and protocol consulting firm in Colorado Springs, Colo., and coauthor with Sue Fox of *Business Etiquette for Dummies* (IDG Books Worldwide, 2001). Writing polite e-mail messages, for example, doesn't take much time and "can have a major impact on the workplace and relationships in the office," says Cunningham.

Second, try following these guidelines from Ethologie when you're composing e-mail messages:

- Write in the same way that you would for any other form of communication. If you wouldn't give lectures that ended with "Do it now," don't use similar language in e-mails.

- Use correct grammar. Bullet points make a message easy to read, but sentence fragments (sentences that do not contain a subject and a verb) do not. And, it's difficult to understand sentences that lack punctuation or capitalization.

- Use the spell check that comes with your e-mail package.

- Make e-mails self-contained with one subject and one message.

- Unless you're engaged in an ongoing conversation, include a greeting/ and or closing, such as, "Hi, Charlene," or "Best wishes, Bob."

- Read messages a couple of times for clarity and tone before hitting the "send" button.

- Change the original subject line if you need to forward a long chain of e-mail to avoid a subject line such as, "FW: FW: RE: FW: RE: Our Meeting."

It's also important to be aware of the management considerations of e-mail use. For instance, the sheer volume of e-mail messages—including mass e-mails that are of little or no concern to the recipients—causes much more frustration among workers than is necessary. Managers shouldn't contribute to the heavy load. "Managers, like everyone else, have to be respectful of other people's time," says Cunningham. Try the following tips to help "manage" your incoming and outgoing e-mail volume:

- Don't use your in-box as a catchall folder. Read items once, then answer immediately, delete or move to a project-specific folder.

- Agree on company acronyms for subject lines, such as AR for action required or MFR for monthly financial report.

- Send group mail sparingly—use only when useful to all recipients. Use "reply all" and "cc" with caution.

- Ask to be removed from distribution lists you do not need to be on.

- Use the "out of office" feature and voice mail message to alert people when you are traveling.

- Before sending an attachment in a particular format, make sure the recipient can open it.

- Avoid sending attachments and graphics to people on the road, unless absolutely necessary. Such attachments can be slow to download. Post large attachments (more than 5 MB) on a web page instead.

- Be specific and helpful. If you send a 30-page attachment, point out critical information on certain pages.

- Respond to your messages as quickly as possible, preferably by the end of the same day.

Then, there's the question of when and when not to rely on e-mail. According to Ethologie, the following do's and don'ts should help you determine when e-mail is appropriate.

Do use e-mail to:

- Set up meetings and prepare attendees. "Thank you for making time to attend Wednesday's board meeting. Before we meet, please review the attached articles about attention deficit disorder in mice and be ready to discuss them."

- Recap spoken conversations. "As we discussed this morning, Jane Smith of ABC Corp. will supply 75 seat cushions for the football game next Saturday."

- Transmit regularly scheduled news feeds, reports, etc.

- Distribute exactly the same information to multiple recipients.

Don't use e-mail to:

- Lambaste a colleague and then copy others on the message. That's tantamount to chewing out someone in front of a room full of his/her peers. Disagreements or discipline are best handled in person or, at least, over the phone.

- Write something you wouldn't want published in the newspaper. Even if you send it to someone you trust, e-mail with sensitive, mean or potentially embarrassing information has a way of being forwarded beyond your original audience.

- Contact someone who sits across the aisle from you unless you're recapping a meeting. If you have a question for discussion, try the old-fashioned approach of speaking to each other.

• Send jokes or forward chain letters.

• Respond to angry colleagues. Pick up the phone or walk into their office.

Remember, while e-mail is a fast, easy and convenient communication tool, it's not always the best choice. Certain kinds of information such as layoffs and firings should be off limits to e-mails. Even Computer Professionals for Social Responsibility, whose 13 board members are scattered throughout North America, turn to the telephone when discussing sensitive matters. "When there are nuances that need to be expressed, and when tone is important, we handle things by conference call because something gets lost on e-mail," explains Coralee Whitcomb, president of the group.

Your E-Mail Checklist

You've just crafted an important e-mail, and you want to ensure that it effectively communicates your message. Check whether your e-mail meets the following criteria for success.

My e-mail message...	Yes	No
1. Reads like a memo, letter or other form of written communication.	❏	❏
2. Contains no errors of grammar, spelling or punctuation.	❏	❏
3. Sticks to one subject and one message about that subject.	❏	❏
4. Has a subject line that briefly captures my message's content.	❏	❏
5. Includes a greeting and a closing.	❏	❏
6. Has the appropriate tone.	❏	❏
7. Doesn't contain acronyms that the recipient won't understand.	❏	❏
8. CC's only additional recipients for whom the message is useful.	❏	❏
9. Doesn't have an overly large attachment that would be difficult for the recipient to download or open.	❏	❏
10. Points out critical information in a lengthy attachment.	❏	❏
11. Doesn't contain sensitive, angry or embarrassing information.	❏	❏
12. Doesn't forward jokes or chain letters.	❏	❏

Quick Tips for Communicating Effectively

- Want to lead important conversations more effectively? Hear what the other person is saying ("Okay, so you think we need to improve productivity."), integrate it into the topic at hand ("So, setting higher sales goals would help us boost productivity.") and say something to move the conversation forward ("How might we go about setting higher sales goals?").

- Interested in becoming a better listener? View verbal exchanges with others as opportunities to gather new and useful information rather than to advocate a position or make judgments about the other person.

- Worried that your boss will "shoot the messenger" if you deliver bad news? Start the conversation by affirming your commitment to keep your boss informed—even if it means delivering difficult or painful news.

- Want to use your communication skills to ensure that your subordinates view you as fair? Tell the truth. Express your desire for employees to succeed. Ask your people for their input on decisions affecting them.

- Wondering what to do when an employee wants to share confidential information with you? Explain that you can't promise confidentiality if the information shared relates to discrimination or harassment, the potential for workplace violence or a possible conflict of interest between you and the company.

- Wondering how to use e-mail most effectively as a communication tool? Write emails in the same way you would any other form of written communication. For example, include a greeting and a closing, use correct grammar and check spelling and tone.

Index

About the Editor
and the Authors

Editor Lauren Keller Johnson has contributed to the series *Business Literacy for Human Resource Professionals* co-published by SHRM and Harvard Business School Press. Based in Cambridge, Massachusetts, Johnson writes for numerous business publications. Her work has appeared in the *Harvard Business Review OnPoint Series, Harvard Management Update* newsletter, *Contingent Workforce Strategies* magazine, *Sloan Management Review*, the *Balanced Scorecard Report*, and *Supply Chain Strategy* newsletter. She has ghostwritten several books and online training modules for managers. Johnson has a master's degree in technical and professional writing from Northeastern University.

Marc Adams is a Winchester, Va.-based journalist specializing in business, finance, and legal affairs. His 34-year career as a writer and editor has included positions as a national correspondent for United Press International and as a senior business writer for The Washington Times. He can be reached at aes@visuallink.com.

Eric Allenbaugh, Ph.D., is an international leadership consultant, executive coach, and keynote speaker on succeeding in business and in life. His major books include *DELIBERATE SUCCESS: Turning Purpose and Passion into Performance Results*, and *WAKE-UP CALLS: You Don't Have to Sleepwalk Through Your Life, Love, or Career*. He is President of Allenbaugh Associates Inc., a leadership development and coaching firm based in Lake Oswego, Oregon, and can be reached via his web site at www.allenbaugh.com.

Linda Wasmer Andrews is a freelance writer in Albuquerque, N.M., who has specialized in health and psychology issues for two decades. She holds a master's degree in health psychology from Capella University and is pursuing a Ph.D. in health psychology through Northcentral University.

Kshanika Anthony, M.A. is a consultant and a manager in PDI's leadership assessment group. For more information on the PROFILOR research, go to www.personneldecisions.com.

William Atkinson has been a full-time business and health writer for more than 25 years, specializing in workplace health and safety. He is author of the book *Eliminate Stress from Your Life Forever: A Simple Program for Better Living*, AMACOM, 2004. He is based in Carterville, Illinois.

Keith Ayers is a consultant and speaker on organizational culture. As CEO of Integro Leadership Institute, he has worked with executive teams across the globe. Ayers is the author of *Engagement is Not Enough: You Need Passionate Employees to Achieve Your Dream*. For more information, go to www.integroleadership.com.

Pamela Babcock is a freelance writer based in the New York City area. She has worked as a reporter for *The Washington Post* and the *News & Observer* in Raleigh, N.C., as well as in corporate communications.

R. Brayton Bowen is the author of *Recognizing and Rewarding Employees* (McGraw-Hill, 2000) and leads The Howland Group, a strategy consulting and change management firm based in Louisville, Ky. A best practice editor and contributing author to *Business: The Ultimate Resource* (Bloomsbury Publishing and Perseus Books, 2002), he currently serves as executive advisor for the McKendree College Center for Business Excellence. He can be reached at Brayton@howlandgroup.com.

Carolyn Brandon is a freelance writer based in suburban, Md., who has worked as a human resource specialist and consultant. She can be reached at pursue11@hotmail.com.

Madelyn Burley-Allen founded Dynamics of Human Behavior in 1972. She is the author of *Listening: The Forgotten Skill* (John Wiley & Sons, 1995), *Managing Assertively: How to Improve Your People Skills* (John Wiley & Sons, 1995) and *Memory Skills in Business* (Crisp Publications, 1988). She can be reached at Dynamics of Human Behavior or dhb8@wimberley-tx.com.

Margaret Butteriss is Vice President, Organizational Consulting with Right Management. She is a highly accomplished executive coach, organization effectiveness, leadership development, and talent management professional. Butteriss can be reached by email at margaret.butteriss@right.com.

Thomas K. Connellan, Ph.D., is chairman of The Connellan Group Inc., a performance and leadership development firm with offices in Orlando, Fla., and Ann Arbor, Mich. He is a frequent keynote speaker at corporate and association meetings and the author of the New York Times bestseller *Bringing Out the Best in Others! 3 Keys for Business Leaders, Educators, Parents, and Coaches* (Bard Press, 2003). He can be reached via his web site at www.tomconnellan.com.

Diana DeLonzor is an internationally recognized management consultant and lead researcher of a major university study investigating chronic lateness. She has been featured in the New York Times, NBC News, NPR Radio, Good Housekeeping Magazine and numerous other international media. Her clients include Fortune 500 companies and government agencies such as Tyco and the State of California. For more information or to request a free anonymous lateness citation, please visit www.neverbelateagain.com.

Catherine Dixon-Kheir is director of organization development at Alignment Strategies Inc., a full-service management consulting company in Washington, D.C. She has led Alignment's Retention of Talent practice for the last ten years. She has spoken on managerial relationships and their impact on retention of talent at numerous events inclusive of the annual conferences for Working Mother Media's Best Companies for Women of Color and. the Society for Human Resource Management.

Paul Falcone is a human resources executive and a best-selling author of five AMACOM books, including *2,600 Phrases for Effective Performance Reviews, The Hiring and Firing Question* and *Answer Book, 96 Great Interview Questions to Ask Before You Hire,* and *101 Sample Write-Ups for Documenting Employee Performance Problems: A Guide to Progressive Discipline and Termination.*

Martha Frase-Blunt is a freelance writer and editor in Martinsburg, WV, specializing in human resources and health care issues. She can be reached at mfrase-blunt@amsa.org.

Lee Gardenswartz and **Anita Rowe** are partners in the management consulting firm of Gardenswartz & Rowe of Los Angeles. Both hold Doctorates of Human Behavior from the United States International University.

Charlotte Garvey is a freelance writer, based in the Washington, D.C., area, who reports on business and environmental issues.

Thad Green, Ph.D., is a former professor of management and is now a consultant and author based in Atlanta. His latest book is *Motivation Management* (Davies-Black, 2000).

Dick Grote is president of Grote Consulting Corporation in Dallas, Texas. He is the author of many books on performance management, including the management classic, *Discipline Without Punishment*, which has recently been published by the American Management Association in an updated second edition. He is also the author of *Forced Ranking: Making Performance Management Work*, published by the Harvard Business School Press.

Kathy Gurchiek is Associate Editor of SHRM's *HR News* online. She has worked at newspapers in Indiana, Illinois, Georgia and Utah; freelanced for media outlets such as The Chicago Tribune and The Associated Press; and holds a master's degree in journalism from Columbia College in Chicago.

Carolyn Hirschman is a business writer in Rockville, Md., who specializes in HR and benefits issues.

Jathan W. Janove is a partner in the law form of Bullard Smith Jernstadt and Wilson, with practices in Portland, Oregon and Salt Lake City. He is an employment law attorney who spends much of his professional time training and coaching managers on dealing with workplace challenges. He is author of the book *Managing to Stay Out of Court* (Berrett-Koehler and SHRM, 2005).

Joelle Jay, Ph.D., is the owner and president of Pillar Consulting LLC (www.pillar-consulting.com), a leadership development firm in Reno, Nev., specializing in leadership and personal effectiveness. She coaches business leaders and executives in achieving success while enhancing the quality of life that keeps them at their best. She can be reached at Joelle@pillar-consulting.com.

Carla Joinson is a freelance writer based in Arlington, Virginia. She specializes in writing about business/management issues, and can be reached by email at joinson@earthllink.net

Deborah A. Keary, SPHR, is Director of Human Resources at the Society for Human Resource Management (SHRM) and former Director of the SHRM Knowledge Center. Keary has written many articles on HR, speaks often to HR professionals on various subjects of interest, and is widely quoted in the media. She holds Master's degrees in Human Resource Management and in Library Science and is certified in both Library Science and as a Senior Human Resource Professional.

Brenda Kowske, Ph.D., is a research consultant for PDI's research division, specializing in development outcome, performance, and systems measurement. For more information on the PROFILOR research, go to www.personneldecisions.com.

Robert N. Llewellyn heads Llewellyn Consulting based in Phoenix, Ariz. He focuses on building business acumen in functional leaders, including HR professionals. His professional experience includes leadership positions in engineering, marketing, business controls and HR/OD. He can be reached at Llewellyn Consulting (www.llew.com).

Amy Maingault, SPHR, is an information specialist in the SHRM Information Center.

Kelly Mollica, Ph.D., SPHR, is a leadership development specialist with The Centre Group, a human asset management firm in Memphis. She is also an Associate Professor of Business at Bethel College. Kelly holds a Ph.D. in business administration with a concentration in organizational behavior and industrial/organizational psychology. Mollica can be reached at kmollica@thecentregroup.com.

Paul Morrow, a graduate from the University of Northern Colorado, worked as a temp for ten years. He currently works for General Electric in the Commercial Finance Department. Morrow has written extensively for television and continues to do so in his spare time.

Dianne Nilsen, Ph.D., is vice president of Leadership Development Products at Personnel Decisions International (PDI). For more information on the PROFILOR research, go to www.personneldecisions.com.

Dawn S. Onley is a Washington, D.C.-based freelance writer. Her work has appeared in The Washington Post, The Star-Ledger, The Philadelphia Daily News, and other major daily newspapers. Ms. Onley can be reached at dawnonley@msn.com.

Laura Gassner Otting is founder and president of the Nonprofit Professionals Advisory Group, a niche consulting firm in Boston that specializes in helping nonprofit organizations with their hiring processes. She can be reached by email at lgo@nonprofitprofessionals.com and via her web site at www.NonprofitProfessionals.com.

Andrea Poe, a writer who divides her time between New York City and Maryland, is the author of hundreds of articles and books on subjects ranging from HR issues to international travel.

William Roiter, Ph.D., is founder and managing partner of Executive Performance Group, a business consulting and executive coaching firm in Newton, Mass. He can be reached at wroiter@executiveperformance. net. Butteriss and Roiter co-authored *Corporate MVPs: Managing Your Company's Most Valuable Performers* (Wiley, 2004).

Brent Roper, SPHR, MBA, JD, is senior manager of human resources for the National Association of Insurance Commissioners, in Kansas City, Mo.

Jonathan A. Segal, Esq., is the Vice Chair of and a partner in the Employment Services Group of Wolf, Block, Schorr and Solis-Cohen LLP, a Philadelphia-based law firm. His practice concentrates on counseling clients, developing policies and programs, and training executives and managers to avoid litigation and unionization. Segal also is the Managing Principal of the Wolf Institute, which provides training to HR professionals, senior executives, managers and in house-counsel.

Robin E. Shea is a member with the Winston-Salem, N.C., office of Constangy, Brooks & Smith, LLC, a national law firm counseling employers since 1946.

Kathryn Tyler is a Wixom, Mich.-based freelance writer and former HR generalist and trainer. She has been writing business-related articles for the last 12 years. She may be contacted via her web site at www.kathryntyler.com.

OTHER BOOKS FROM SHRM

Additional titles from the Society for Human Resource
Management (SHRM®)

*Building Profit through Building People: Making Your Workforce the
Strongest Link in the Value-Profit Chain*
> By Ken Carrig and Patrick M. Wright

*The Comprehensive, All-in-One HR Operating Guide:
539 ready-to-adapt human resource letters, memos, procedures,
practices, forms…and more*
> By R. J. Landry

Diverse Teams at Work: Capitalizing on the Power of Diversity
> By Lee Gardenswartz and Anita Rowe

The Essential Guide to Federal Employment Laws
> By Lisa Guerin and Amy DelPo

HIPAA Privacy Source Book
> By William S. Hubbartt

Harvard Business School Press/SHRM
Business Literacy for HR Professionals Series: *The Essentials of…*
> *Corporate Communications and Public Relations*
> *Finance and Budgeting*
> *Managing Change and Transition*
> *Negotiation*
> *Power, Influence, and Persuasion*
> *Project Management*
> *Strategy*

HR Source Book Series

    Employment Termination Source Book
    By Wendy Bliss, J.D., SPHR and Gene R. Thornton, Esq., PHR

    HIPAA Privacy Source Book
    By William S. Hubbartt, SPHR, CCP

    Hiring Source Book
    By Cathy Fyock, CAP, SPHR

    Performance Appraisal Source Book
    By Mike Deblieux

    Trainer's Diversity Source Book
    By Jonamay Lambert, M.A. and Selma Myers, M.A.

Human Resource Essentials: Your Guide to Starting and Running the HR Function
    By Lin Grensing-Pophal, SPHR

Outsourcing Human Resources Functions: How, Why, When and When Not to Contract for HR Services
    By Mary F. Cook and Scott B. Gildner

Practical HR Series

    Legal, Effective References: How to Give and Get Them
    By Wendy Bliss, J.D., SPHR

    Investigating Workplace Harassment: How to Be Fair, Thorough, and Legal
    By Amy Oppenheimer, J.D., and Craig Pratt, MSW, SPHR

    Proving the Value of HR: How and Why to Calculate ROI
    By Jack J. Phillips, Ph.D. and Patricia Pulliam Phillips, Ph.D.